Staying Alive!

A special *"Thank You"* to Chris Byrne
for inspiring the title of this book *"Staying Alive!"*

-- I have no doubt that the knowledge gained from reading your book saved me from being seriously injured and possibly killed when I was recently the victim of a knife yielding armed robber.
-- I say thanks again, and strongly recommend your book to anyone who is interested in "Staying Alive!"

Staying Alive!

Your
CRIME PREVENTION
Guide

By

Richard A. Fike, Sr.

With Illustrations by Doug Atkins
Photographs by Gary Cartner

ACROPOLIS BOOKS LTD.

WASHINGTON, D.C.

ACROPOLIS BOOKS LTD.
2311 Calvert St., N.W. #300
Washington, D.C. 20008

Attention: Schools and Corporations
ACROPOLIS books are available at quantity discounts with bulk purchase for educational, business, or sales promotional use. For information, please write to:
Acropolis Books Ltd., 2311 Calvert St., N.W. #300
Washington, D.C. 20008

Library of Congress Cataloging-in-Publication Data

Fike, Richard A., 1955 Sr.-
  Staying alive! your crime prevention guide
  p. cm.
  Includes bibliographical references and index (p. 216).
  ISBN 0-87491-970 :$19.95 hc;
    1. Crime Prevention---United States--Juvenile literature.
  2. Violent crimes--United States--Prevention--Juvenile literature.
  I. Title
HV9950.F55 1994   94-14567
362.88--dc20   CIP

Are there Acropolis Books you want but cannot find in your stores or library?
You can get any Acropolis book in print by simply sending title and retail price to ACROPOLIS BOOKS LTD., 2311 Calvert St., NW #300, Washington, D.C. 20008. Please add $3.50 to cover shipping costs. Credit cards accepted. For faster service, please call toll-free 1-800-451-7771.

Dedication

To my children, Leah, Rick Jr. and Sara.

Acknowledgments

As with any project which requires the assistance of my friends, family and professional associates, I wish to express my appreciation for their support and patience.

First to my publisher, Mr. Al Hackl, for his part in educating families worldwide in methods to prevent and combat crime through the publication of this book. To my talented friend, Doug Atkins, for his valuable time and superb illustrations, and to my trusted friend and veteran police office, Jim Miller, for his assistance in compiling valuable crime statistics. I also want to thank James T. McBride, Chief of Police and Director of Security & Safety at Lakeland Community College, Mentor, Ohio for his valuable insight into his concept of Crimeaphobia. I want to thank my wife, Linda, and my children for being patient with me, and lastly to the students, teachers and parents of my martial arts school, the Madison Combined Martial Arts Association for also being patient and understanding of my occasional absence while writing this project.

Contents

Are You Afflicted With Crimeaphobia?

crimeaphobia *(krīm-a-fōbēa)* **1.** a term coined in 1983 by Chief James T. McBride, Mentor, Ohio. **2.** the fear of criminal victimization of attack. **3.** symptoms range from simple apprehension or anxiety, to feelings of terror, or panic at the mere thought of victimization. [Chief McBride is also Director of Security and Safety at the Lakeland Community College in Mentor, Ohio.]

If you are afraid to go out of your house alone, worry excessively about the safety of your children, or of the idea of going out alone into the dark, then chances are that you are afflicted with Crimeaphobia.

Most people are not concerned about crime until it strikes someone close to them, their family, friends, or neighbors. When crime reaches out and points its crooked finger in our direction, we quickly realize how vulnerable we really are.

If we allow the mere threat of crime to dominate our thoughts, then we become victims of our own making. We lock ourselves behind closed doors, we trust no one, and virtually become slaves of the "fear" of crime.

For many, Crimeaphobia may be just as emotionally disturbing as surviving an actual mugging, or beating at the hands of a criminal.

The Figgie Report on the Fear of Crime—America Afraid, published in 1980, and The Figgie Report Part VI—The Business of Crime, published in 1988, help illustrate the crimeaphobia theory. Figgie researchers found that "four out of 10 Americans are highly fearful of becoming victims of violent crime, such as murder, rape, robbery or assault. Further, four out of ten Americans feel unsafe in their everyday environment, their homes, their neighborhoods, their business districts and shopping centers."

*What can you, your family and your neighborhood do to fight this disease of fear? Happily, **Staying Alive! Your Crime Prevention Guide** provides an easy-to-follow prescription.*

In the pages that follow, you will find practical, step-by-step instructions on how to cope with the various crime situations. It is everybody's guide to crime prevention. It will help us take back our streets, our schools and our neighborhoods!

-Richard A. Fike, Sr.

1

Much Crime Can Be Prevented

Do You Invite Crime by the Way You Walk...Look?

The amount of crime we are experiencing in the United States today is frightening. It is especially disheartening to hear how much of it could have been prevented if only the necessary precautions had been taken. We all run the risk of becoming a victim at least once during our lifetime; for many of us, the odds are even greater.

Someone is murdered in the United States every 22 minutes, robbed every 47 seconds and seriously assaulted every 28 seconds. It seems that at least one newspaper story appears every day about a rape, assault, kidnapping, or similar crime in each of our neighborhoods. Perhaps you even know the victim involved. When we hear about a violent crime, our first reaction is one of disgust. Then we silently thank the good Lord that it did not involve a member of our own family.

But what if it had? What if your son or daughter had been attacked, injured, or even killed? Feelings of anger, rage, and helplessness quickly follow. Now you have to become involved. How guilty would you feel if it were too late to do something to save your child? Unfortunately, this after-the-fact attitude, rather than the attitude of prevention, seems to prevail.

In many cases, people blame society, or express outrage that the police failed to prevent certain crimes. We cannot expect law enforcement agencies in our communities to stop all crime in its tracks.

It's always easier to look back and point out what went wrong than to look into the future to know who will be the next victim, or what the risks are in each of our lives. We can, however, develop the proper attitude towards the prevention of crime. This leads to the next step: taking action against crime, through organized and systematic preventatives.

Crime affects literally every segment of society. It can strike out at anyone at any time. We cannot choose when we would like to be attacked. There is no taking a number, and there is never a "better" time to be assaulted. Study the following chart. Its statistics can give you an idea of the incidence of murder, robbery, and aggravated assaults in the area where you live.

The High Cost of Crime

Statistics released from the Federal Bureau of Investigation (FBI) disclosed that during 1992 there was a total of 12,505,900 property crimes committed across the United States, a rate of one every three seconds.

The dollar loss from major crimes nationwide resulting from burglary (one every 11 seconds) was $3.8 billion; larceny-theft (one every four seconds) equaled $3.8 billion; motor vehicle theft (one every 20 seconds) reached $7.6 billion; and robbery (one every 47 seconds) totaled $565.7 million.

During 1992, there was a total of 23,760 murders and non-negligent manslaughter offenses, 109,060 forcible rapes, 672,480 robberies, 1,126,970 aggravated assaults, 2,979,900 burglaries, 7,915,200 offenses of larceny-theft and 1,610,800 incidents of motor vehicle theft.

Arrests By Age Group

Information compiled by the FBI discloses that 61.3 percent of all arrests in 1992 for auto theft was listed to persons between the ages of 15 and 24.

Persons under the age of 20 accounted for 56 percent of all arrests for the crime of arson, and 39 percent of the arrests for driving under the influence of intoxicants involved persons between the ages of 20 and 29.

Records, therefore, indicate that persons between the ages of 15 and 24, followed by those 25 to 29, were involved in a disproportionately high number of arrests, which has a direct impact on the financial losses paid out by insurers. As a result, those of us not directly affected by one particular crime very often find ourselves indirectly affected by rising insurance premiums and other related costs attributed to the overall incidence of crime.

The Key to Survival is Awareness

This book will help you avoid becoming one of those statistics. The key to survival is to establish the necessary safeguards and take the preventive measures to eliminate or at least limit the opportunity for crime.

You can become difficult to attack, or simply not worth the attacker's trouble. As selfish as it may sound, you want the criminal to look elsewhere for a victim. Former criminals, as well as those on the streets today, will tell you that their targets all tend to exhibit certain weak characteristics. It's common sense to choose a target that you feel confident you can defeat.

In many cases, victims often attract or invite assault because of the way they walk, talk, and dress. Walking with your head down, unsure or uncoordinated in your movements, signifies a possible lack of confidence. This could happen when walking through a new shopping plaza, or an unfamiliar city block — your body language can alert potential muggers to approaching prey.

The reverse can be true of a person who walks with a smooth, even stride. Coordination increases with relaxation. Relaxation increases with confidence. Add the fact that this person's head is erect, and that he is aware of all activity in his vicinity, and you now have a person who would not be considered an easy mark. The assailant alert to these positive body cues would probably decide to look elsewhere for a more susceptible target.

Developing and maintaining a positive and confident attitude is really not difficult. When you understand and analyze the activities that surround you, you'll find that your confidence grows and radiates. This positive attitude is a plus for you, and a minus for the criminal.

Crime does not always choose its victims by their affluence. It often strikes out at the first person in its path — some poor soul in the wrong place at the right time. This is why we must learn to expect the unexpected if we want to be prepared to face any possible situation.

Although most of the criminals who infect our society choose a life of crime freely, in many cases society is to blame. What deters the criminal from his wrongdoings? In some cases, it can be the establishment, strictly enforcing the law. In other cases, social reform affects each member of that society. Threat of strict punishment can prevent crime in some cases, and a return to crime in others. Unfortunately, crime can never be completely eliminated. We must accept this fact, and prepare to meet it whenever it should come to call.

This book provides recommendations and procedures for you to use in developing effective measures or strengthening already established procedures.

It's Up To You To Get Involved

By choosing to read this book, you have already shown a concern for crime prevention. The next step is to apply what you have learned. Nobody is going to do it for you.

Three Priorities

The guidelines established in this book follow a simple, logical set of priorities:

Priority I: Education and Motivation. You're never too old to learn. You're never too young to be responsible. Get involved and make a difference in your community today. Spread the word that there are things people can do to protect themselves, their families, homes and neighborhoods.

Through education, you will learn to recognize potential threats before they happen and learn how to deal with them. Through involvement, you can take satisfaction in knowing that you have made a difference. Motivate your family to get involved as well. Crime prevention should be a never-ending family priority that nurtures our children to grow into responsible, concerned citizens who do more than simply talk about crime prevention. After all, if parents refuse to get involved, then why should their children?

Priority II: Options. The criminal always determines his options before making his move. Have you? What are your options during a crisis? Have you really taken the time to think about what you would do, and how you would do it, when faced with a criminal? You are not helpless. Don't become a victim. Be a hassle. Change the rules that the criminal plays by, and send out a message loud and clear that you're no longer weak and vulnerable.

Priority III: Apply your education. As you read through this book, highlight each chapter as it pertains to you and your family. Review each chapter in detail with your family, church group or school system. Encourage questions as well as recommendations from everyone, and remember that as an adult, you must lead by example. If you fail to place importance on keeping the back door locked, will your children? You can make a difference!

2

Teenage Violence: Guns, Gangs, Drugs & Carjackings

T eenage violence is spreading across the globe at an alarming rate. Too much time, too much money and too much talk have been exhausted dealing with this problem after it occurs, and we are quickly losing the battle to contain it. It seems everywhere that you look, in every city and community, you will find an increase in teen deaths through suicide, alcoholism, drug abuse and gang violence.

Juveniles who know that they are automatically looked at as "hands off," receive a slap on the wrist for violent crimes which include murder. Numerous incidents of premeditated murder perpetrated by 15-year-olds seem to occur almost daily. Shouldn't a juvenile be charged and sentenced as an adult when circumstances show that he willfully and knowingly committed a crime? Shouldn't parents of convicted juveniles be held accountable for the damage their children do? These issues must be dealt with.

Children are being shot, stabbed and murdered every day, and what's frightening is that much of this crime is being committed by children. When apprehended, the child appears before a juvenile justice system that allows him to walk free.

Today's juveniles are rarely punished for their actions, and, like adults, they rarely respond to rehabilitation. Quite literally, there's a war going on out there, and our youth are either fighting against it, fighting with it, or dying because of it.

We have to treat juvenile violence as a disease, and we must work together to find the cure. As a society, we must immediately develop and implement effective preventive measures that will keep the infection of teen violence from spreading.

Guns, Homicide and Suicide

Undoubtedly the most violent acts committed by children involve the use of firearms. Over 75 percent of juvenile homicides in 1991-92, and over half of juvenile suicides reported in the United States, were committed with guns. Kids think guns are cool, and when it comes to power, they're the ultimate ego trip. Using a gun to commit a crime is considered the rite of passage for some gang members, and, with a gun, they believe they can demand respect and afford an affluent lifestyle that can be obtained and maintained only with the possession and occasional use of a firearm.

In 1992, over 15,377 murders were recorded involving the use of firearms. Of these victims, 5000 were young adults under the age of 19, or the equivalent of 15 children a day. Thousands more are wounded by firearms each year. Gunshot wounds are the fifth leading cause of accidental death among children 14 years of age, and are also the foremost cause of death among black teenage males.

While not restricted to any one particular race or sex, suicide by firearms is common among white suburban families. A variety of factors can prompt adolescents to kill themselves, such as parental divorce, broken love relationships, sexual abuse by a parent or the death of a friend. Availability of a gun makes the decision to end a life much easier and faster.

Neighborhood and schoolyard arguments that once erupted into a wrestling match or occasional bloody nose now end in gunfire. Drive-by shootings are frequent and innocent people are being killed. Nobody is safe from the automatic weapons fire delivered from a speeding car, which guarantees death to anyone standing at the wrong place at the wrong time.

Gangs

The word "gang" can be defined as "a group of people working or acting together." However, the gangs that we need to be concerned with are those groups of people who engage in violent criminal activity. Most violent gangs seek to identify and control territory or "turf," and will openly oppose other gangs, as well as police and citizens group efforts to eliminate them. Competition is fierce for controlling the drug market, extortion and "protection."

Gangs, not unlike terrorists, employ both violence and/or the threat of violence to intimidate and control their victim(s). In most cases, the victim is a community or a specific block within that community, and often there is another rival gang seeking to move in and take over.

Although different in appearance, most gangs share some common explanations for their existence:

- Almost always a product of impoverished urban neighborhoods.
- Exist in areas that suffer from high unemployment.
- Originate and survive in areas of high population.
- Operate in areas experiencing high crime.

History reflects that at one time the primary victims of a gang were rival gang members. Today everyone is subject to gang violence. Every day we hear of another innocent bystander who was killed by a stray bullet fired from a passing car.

Gangs derive their power from their membership and from the weapons they carry. Banding together in an organized group, much like a pack of wild animals on the prowl, gang members feel strong and powerful. For the most part, they could never be as threatening individually. Generally, they are failures in society — school drop-outs, drug dealers and punks. They have few friends, have nowhere to go, and, for obvious reasons, receive no respect from society. One way to gain respect and a feeling of worth is to join a gang.

Together, gang members feel secure, gain companionship and a sense of belonging. For some, the only way they can survive is through the support of a gang. Ironically, many of the gang-related killings are committed from within the gang itself, and not from rival gangs as believed.

Most new prospective members must prove themselves worthy through acts determined by those already in the gang before they are accepted.

Almost all gangs can be identified by their distinctive markings, clothing, and tattoos; however, they are prepared to change their looks and locations to avoid apprehension by local police or targeting by a rival gang.

Drugs and Money

Gang membership offers protection and support to its members. How can society expect a child to remain motivated to stay in school and do the right thing when all he hears at home is how the unemployment check stopped coming, how the family has no medical or health insurance, and how Mom and Dad are getting a divorce? The family structure that he needs no longer exists at home, so he finds it within his new support group, the gang.

Freedom and opportunity to do what he wants, when he wants, is attractive to a confused, desperate juvenile. Why should he go to work for minimum wage at a fast food restaurant or car wash when he can make a thousand dollars a day dealing drugs? A new car, a gold-plated watch and a chrome-plated 9mm are attainable through the skills he learns as a gang member.

Some gangs are taking in a weekly income of a million dollars by dealing in cocaine. Make no mistake of it, gangs are in business to make money, and children are being manipulated to take all the risks. It's good business to employ juveniles to deal drugs, because, if apprehended, they are quickly released back into society and onto the streets. "After all, they are just children and should not be held accountable for their actions." Most juvenile first-offenders walk free from any serious punishment from the courts and thus quickly learn how to play the game. It becomes very easy to literally get away with murder and receive no punishment for their actions.

Juvenile gang members often reside at home with their families, but come and go as they please. While not condoning it, some parents look the other way as their children participate in gang activity, especially if they are bringing home extra dollars. Until the court systems improve, or until parents are held accountable for their children, this problem will continue to grow and become more difficult to resolve.

Carjacking, the Bump & Run and the Smash & Grab

Though accounting for only a small percentage of motor vehicle thefts reported, carjackings, also known as the "bump and run," are occurring more and more across the United States. Carjackings usually occur when a vehicle comes to a stop at a traffic light or stop sign in an isolated or abandoned part of town. Carjackers look for a vehicle with only one person in it, then roll into the back of the victim. Once the concerned driver exits to inspect for damage or injuries, the carjacker or his accomplice quickly jumps into the victim's vehicle and drives away. Unfortunately, many victims are injured or murdered during carjacking.

In another version, some criminals will intentionally set up a victim for a rear-end collision by driving at a controlled speed, then, at the right moment, slamming on their brakes forcing the victim to ram their car from behind. Once again the plan has been set in motion, and both the vehicle and driver are at the mercy of the carjackers.

More frequent in some areas is the "smash and grab" technique. Here the criminal waits for his victim to come to a stop, then quickly approaches, asking for spare change. Or he immediately begins washing the vehicle's windows, hoping to delay the driver in order to get a peek inside. If something is within reach, such as a purse, a radio or car phone, the criminal will smash the window and grab whatever he can. Here again, get in his way and you could end up injured or worse.

If someone approaches your vehicle, keep your windows rolled up, even in the summer, and keep all doors locked. Act confident, and if you have some type of effective chemical deterrent, mace or even hair spray, open the window just a crack, and point the spray at your would-be attacker. It might buy you enough time to escape with your car and your life.

You must always be prepared for the unexpected, especially when traveling into a high crime area. It's important to commit mentally to survival during a carjacking. The criminal has already committed to taking whatever you have, and if that means injuring you in the process, so be it. If he wants your car or your purse, there is little that you can do without risking a violent confrontation, short of driving away or driving over your attacker.

If you suspect that you have been set up in a bump and run, never exit your vehicle. Observe the driver and passengers in the other vehicle, and record the make and license number. Allow the other driver to approach your vehicle, but ask him, with the window open just a crack, for his license and insurance information first. If he refuses or acts strange, tell him, or wave to him, to follow you to the nearest police station or occupied public area to handle the incident. It's illegal to leave the scene of an accident, but most police officers will tell you, especially in a high crime area, if the situation is suspicious, attempt to safely drive away to the nearest public area to exchange insurance and related information. Never get out of your vehicle unless there are other responsible witnesses nearby. Use good judgment and common sense to avoid exposing yourself or your family to possible danger. I would rather explain my decision for leaving the scene of an accident to a police officer, than try to talk my way out of a carjacking with a drug-crazed punk with a pistol.

Tips to Avoid a Carjacking or Smash & Grab

- Never travel alone into an area that is isolated or unfamiliar to you.
- Never drive into a suspicious or obviously dangerous situation.
- Always remain alert, aware of your surroundings.
- Never display valuables in your vehicle that would attract or invite a possible smash and grab.
- If followed by another vehicle, never drive to your residence (including hotel). Drive to a public location, police or fire station.
- While driving, never get into a dispute or argument with another vehicle driver. Give him

the right of way, move to the slow lane and let the hothead pass by. He could have a gun beside him.

- When approaching a stop, anticipate your position and allow sufficient spacing between you and other vehicles for an emergency escape.

- If cut off in front, or rammed from behind, use common sense to determine the legitimacy of the accident. If you suspect foul play or fear for your life, drive away from the area and directly to a police or fire station for assistance.

- When parking your vehicle, look for a lighted spot. If possible, park in a facility that utilizes a security guard or parking attendant; however, never give attendant any keys other than those for the vehicle.

- If threatened with a weapon, cooperate. If forced to exit your vehicle, attempt to escape. Never try to drive away unless you are certain you can do so safely, or in the event that no other safe alternative exists.

What Can Be Done?

We must help children understand and learn how to manage their anger; however, keeping guns out of the hands of the children who feel anger is going to be very difficult. Until we firmly control the availability of guns on the streets, we will never control juvenile crime. Currently, national reports indicate that seven out of 10 murders in the United States were committed with handguns, and that the majority of the crimes that were committed were with firearms that were illegally obtained.

Gun control is a controversy all to itself, but the majority of Americans feel that some form of gun control should exist. Enter the Brady Bill, which mandates a waiting period. Unfortunately, the juveniles who really want a gun know how and where to get one, and without any waiting period. Parents have to take a more active role in educating, supervising and enforcing juvenile offenders.

Suggestions for Schools

- Violence Prevention curricula that help juveniles understand the consequences for their actions, while removing the "glamorous" tough-guy image associated with firearms, gangs and drugs.

- Group discussion to help peers understand and deal with the fear of firearms and shootings in their neighborhoods and schools.

- Firearm safety courses, especially for those families who possess a firearm in their home.

- Security escorts for visitors.

- Offender diversion courses that are designed to provide counseling, violence prevention classes, disciplinary boot camps, and trips to local jails help to prevent the first-time offender from escalating to a life of crime. The biggest advantage in this type of program is that it gives the offender time to think and evaluate his past and present situation, thereby giving him a second chance to rejoin a free society.

- Peer mediation groups help negotiate disputes, and teach ways to communicate and resolve problems without violence. Selected students are trained to be mediators by a certified staff.

- Don't rely on gun control alone to solve the problem. Guns don't kill. People with guns kill.

- School systems should install metal detectors, practice emergency disaster drills, set up security patrols and closed-circuit television.

- Concentrate on developing character. Reward positive performance and reinforce responsible, mature behavior.

- Establish support group organizations that place a strong priority on providing role models, building character, leadership and team cooperation. Experience has found activities such as the martial arts, scouting and church clubs teach and reinforce positive development.

- Emphasize how a good reputation as well as a bad reputation will follow children through their lives.

Accountability: Who Should Be Responsible?

Juvenile laws were written to protect children. Children are not expected to be as responsible as adults, or to make adult decisions. But should society allow children, who demonstrate that they think and act as adults, to be released from their responsibility to obey the laws of the same society that protects them? Our juvenile courts and probation departments are full of young adults who want the freedoms and benefits of adults, but do not want to accept the responsibilities that go along with being an adult. Can you have it both ways? Courts across the nation are reviewing, rewriting and redefining what constitutes juvenile accountability.

One area of difficulty is assigning punishment, which presumes that the offender is responsible for the acts that were committed. In our society, the courts do not punish those who are judged to be incompetent or mentally ill. Juveniles as a rule are not expected to be fully responsible. Although questionable, when it comes to breaking the law, they receive protection from adult punishment.

It is obvious the court systems are struggling to resolve the accountability issue of juvenile justice, both for the good of our youth and for the good of society. Somewhere there has to be a balance.

Alternatives to Violence

Controlling the problem of teen violence should first begin within the home environment. It is all parents' responsibility to raise their children to respect the laws of our society. Many parents are failing to supervise and educate their children to be honest, law abiding citizens. In fact, many parents expect someone else to raise their children for them.

The next line of education and supervision falls within the jurisdiction of local school systems. Teachers need to be able to communicate with their students and offer them nonviolent solutions to their problems. Students need to learn how to communicate with each other, how to share their problems, their fears, and their future. Teachers who are concerned with education will continue to seek new, more effective methods to motivate and educate the youth in their classrooms.

One teacher who has done just that is Mrs. Carolyn J. Staudt, a physics teacher at Copley High School in Copley, Ohio. She is project director for several successful alternative educational programs that have stimulated and motivated students to a new level of learning and nonviolence. As a result, her programs have been adopted and initiated at schools across the country.

Basically, she has developed and coordinated specialized alternative educational programs which have been approved by the local school district and funded through grants and corporate sponsors. These programs have proven to be extremely effective in molding students into future scientists, teachers and responsible citizens.

Projects encompass all the areas of science and technology, from machinery and physics to biology. Students learn useful skills such as computers, public speaking, team work, effective leadership and communication, then apply them in actual hands-on exercises.

Students don't have time to get into trouble. They are too busy learning and performing exciting experiments to go looking for trouble; however, if a disagreement or argument occurs, the program is designed to make the participants supervise and resolve any problems themselves. They learn to communicate and work out their problems and differences together in order for the experiments to be successful.

In the end, the students gain a sense of accomplishment and pride in their own learning that contributes to mature behavior. Teachers and students work together to accomplish a variety of tasks. Separate from the academic achievements that are obvious, the relationships established between student and teacher, and student and student, play a vital role in our search for alternatives to teen violence.

For information about Mrs. Staudt's programs, write or call:

Carolyn J. Staudt
3807 Ridgewood Road
Copley, Ohio 44321
(216) 666-9205.

Recognizing Threats In Your Home Environment

E velyn left her garden apartment to run out for some charcoal to barbecue some steaks.

"I don't need to lock the sliding glass door out back," she thought to herself. "I'll only be gone a few minutes."

An hour later, Evelyn returned to a ransacked apartment. Gone were her camera, stereo, video recorder, home computer, the steaks and her hibachi! Luckily, everything except the steaks was marked with her social security number, so if any of the stolen items are recovered, she should get them back. But Evelyn will never again leave the back door open for "just a few minutes."

Throughout most of our daily routine, we find ourselves or members of our family, in, or between, one of four basic environments: *home, work, school* or *recreational*. By carefully studying these environments on an individual basis, we can identify the special threats and vulnerabilities that are unique to each of the four, and establish effective preventive procedures against them. Once prevention has been instituted, we can move in a positive direction to create a far more controlled environment than previously thought. We are prepared to handle the situations that arise by being knowledgeable of the crises that are likely to affect us in each environment.

It's next to impossible to know where crime will strike. Naturally, if we knew, we could avoid it. Because, however, we cannot always avoid crime, we must be prepared to deter or stop it. To do so requires sound prevention. It may also call for the application of defensive tactics.

We are all concerned about securing our homes or apartments from criminals. After all, we like to think of our homes as our castles, affording us safety and protection from the elements.

Most of us are aware of the need to protect our homes, but seldom do we actually take necessary precautionary measures. Many feel that it's too costly; others simply don't take the time or make the effort to establish minimal preventive measures. It's one thing to come home and discover that someone has stolen your television set and stereo, make out a police report, and call the insurance company. It's another thing altogether to be caught at home when the criminal breaks through your back door. What if someone tries to break into your house while your children and the babysitter are there? Who is this intruder? What should you do to deter him?

There are two main types of burglars. One is the professional thief, who spends much time studying, or "casing" your residence. He looks for your patterns of activity, and selects the prime time to enter. In most cases, the victims provide the burglar with easy access through unlocked doors or windows, or even by leaving a key under the mat. The professional will generally escape unnoticed, never to be caught.

The amateur is, in most cases, a juvenile who needs quick money. He moves directly into the residence, often by breaking windows or doors. This amateur thief is usually very nervous and clumsy as he searches for money or things that can be sold quickly, such as a stereo, camera or television set.

In most cases, the amateur is more dangerous. When surprised by the resident, he may panic, and shoot or stab. The professional is likely to flee before confronting an occupant.

The Criminal's Priorities — Time & Concealment

Time and concealment are the two main priorities to the criminal. Slow him down, or light up the shadows in which he works, and he will go elsewhere. He does not want to be observed or apprehended; therefore any target or opportunity that looks like a hassle is usually bypassed. Make it tough on the criminal; don't invite him inside with your family.

Internal and External Protection

If you're looking for a home to rent or buy, drive through the area and talk with neighbors and business people. Do this at night, and on weekends, to see what type of activity exists.

Read the following checklist to determine how vulnerable your home or apartment is. Once you identify the weaknesses, you can begin to make corrections.

If you live in an apartment, contact the manager or landlord to assist in the survey. You might even remind him that by increasing safeguards, he can probably save on his insurance premiums!

Residential Survey Questions

1. How much security currently exists?
2. How effective is existing security?
3. What crime has already occurred?
4. How much/what type of crime exists in this neighborhood?
5. How long does it take for local police, fire, and rescue services to arrive?
6. How much can you afford to spend to increase existing home security?

External Home Security Checklist

1. What is your location in relation to neighbors or businesses? Establish complete boundaries and perimeters of residences. Use photos, illustrations, maps.

2. Is your house or apartment number visible from the street, 24 hours a day, for emergency service? If not, consider placing it in plain view.

3. What type of landscaping surrounds your residence?

    - Does it block the view of the driveway or garage?
    - Do bushes, hedges, or fences provide cover for a criminal near windows, doors, or sidewalks?
    - Do trees, existing buildings, fences, or flower trellises provide access onto a roof, ledge, or balcony?

4. What barriers border your residence?

    - Are there fences? Do they have gates that secure and operate effectively?
    - Are there walls from other buildings?
    - Are there natural barriers such as hedges?
    - Are there vehicles (e.g., trucks) parked nearby that afford entry over perimeter barriers?

5. What type of lighting exists?

    - Are there street lights? Do they work?
    - Do existing lights provide complete and adequate coverage to all entrances, exits, parking lots, driveways, etc.?
    - Have you considered lights that turn on automatically at dusk, and off at dawn?
    - Is there an alternate light source or back-up lighting system?

6. Are there any additional buildings or sheds, and are they secured properly?

7. Where are the external fuse or power boxes?

8. Are fuse/power boxes locked securely?

9. Is the telephone cable accessible from the ground?

10. Does the garage door open, close, and lock properly?

11. Are all unused doors and windows permanently locked?

12. Are all ladders and lawn furniture secured properly?

13. Is there a guard dog?
    - Is the guard dog secured?
    - Is the guard dog protected from the weather?
    - Are there "Beware of Dog" signs posted?

14. Are the vehicles parked outside your residence locked, and the windows rolled up tight?

15. Are hidden access keys located outside in obvious locations?

16. If female, and living alone, is your full name (preceded by Ms., Miss, or Mrs.) listed on your mail box? Use your first and middle initials only, with your last name, in order not to alert would-be criminals that you are alone.

17. Are keys for all external locks marked and maintained in a safe and secured location inside the residence?

Internal Home Security Checklist

1. Does each room, including hallways and stairs, have an adequate lighting system? Are timers used when on vacation?

2. Is there an auxiliary lighting back-up system?

3. Are flashlights and charged batteries stored in each room? Consider disposable flashlights.

4. Does each room have window blinds or shades?

5. Is there a first-aid kit, with a manual, in the house?

6. Are internal doors equipped with locking devices?

7. Can these doors be opened from outside the room in the event a child is locked in?

8. Are smoke alarms installed and working?

9. Is there a fire exit plan? Are all residents aware of it?

10. If residing in an apartment complex, do main outer doors lock, requiring resident keys to open them?

11. Are there fire extinguishers where needed?

12. Where is the internal fuse/power box located?

    - Is the fuse/power box reachable?
    - Are extra fuses available?

13. Do all telephones have emergency phone numbers (police, fire and rescue, poison control center) posted on or near them?

14. Are weapons stored inside the home?

    - Are all family members aware of weapons and their location?
    - Are weapons stored in a safe location to prevent accidental discovery?

15. Is there a complete inventory list of all property, with extra copies stored in a safe deposit box and with the insurance company?

16. Is there a security room designated to provide a hiding place for family members?

17. Does the security room contain all the necessary emergency supplies?

18. Is there a security safe or fire-resistant steel box for important papers, documents, and valuables?

    - Who knows where the safe is?
    - Who knows the safe combination?

Apartment/College Campus Tips

1. Who else has keys that will fit your residence or room?

2. Will management/college re-key your doors?

3. If not, will management/college let you pay for this service? (It is worth it.)

4. How secure are existing door and window locks?

5. Are all stairways, hallways, and surrounding property well lighted?

6. Where is the laundry room? Is it well lighted and secured?

7. Does your apartment or campus building have an emergency fire alarm? Does it work? Where is the fire exit?

Locking Devices

No home can be completely burglar-proofed, but you can reduce the chances of a break-in. Most residences can be entered with little or no force. As mentioned earlier, many people go to great lengths to obtain expensive locking systems, only to leave their doors and windows unlocked.

Some homes are secured with only a spring-latch door lock that can be pried open within seconds. Check your locks by opening the door and locking the lock device (usually by pushing in a button). Next, with your finger, try to push in the bolt that locks into the door frame when it's closed. If the bolt slides back into the door, you have a spring-latch lock. If at all possible, replace this lock with a deadbolt lock, or even better, add a deadbolt in addition to the existing lock.

If your door is fitted improperly to the door frame (leaving a narrow gap), there is the possibility of a criminal popping, jimmying, or prying the locking bolt from the doorstrike. If possible, replace door frames with new metal frames, and old doors with solid hardwood or metal, especially if you are building your home.

If the lock bolt and the lock strike are strong, the criminal sometimes attempts to pry the door off its hinges. Check to insure that hinge screws are not stripped and that they are tightly and properly secured. In most cases, it's probably very easy to lift the hinge pin from the hinge and enter through this side of the door. So be sure to keep all hinges facing inward, with the door swinging in. You can improve door security if you remove the center screw from each side of the existing hinge, drill each hole to a depth of ½ inch, and place a headless screw or pin on one side (Figure 3-1). When the door is closed, the end of the screw or pin will seat itself into the empty screw hole. If the hinge pins are removed, the door will still be bolted to the frame.

Figure 3-1

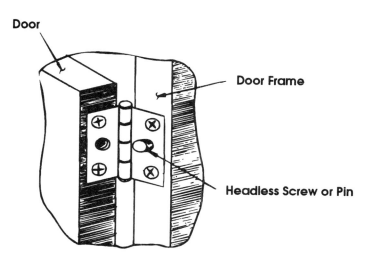

Door

Door Frame

Headless Screw or Pin

Deadbolts offer just about the highest degree of security you can expect, short of Fort Knox. Deadbolt locks can only be opened by a key or a key-turn knob. There are different qualities of deadbolts on the market today, so it's important to choose one made of case-hardened steel, which resists cutting.

You can reinforce the door-frame strike to provide maximum strength. The strike plate should be attached to the door frame with screws at least three inches long. Make sure that the bolt, when locked, seats at least five-eighths of an inch in the doorjamb. Also be sure that the cylinder of the lock has a steel guard (a ring around the key section) that's tapered around the key slot to keep it from being wrenched off (Figure 3-2). Secure the lock cylinder with five or six pin tumblers to provide more resistance against picking, although very few residences are entered by the lock-picking method. Lock-picking requires a certain amount of skill, but even the best pickers struggle when picking an old, worn, or damaged lock, so this technique is seldom used.

Figure 3-2

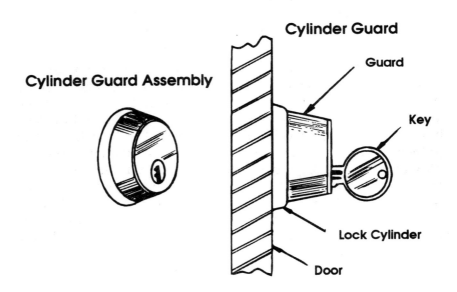

Cylinder Guard

Cylinder Guard Assembly

Guard

Key

Lock Cylinder

Door

Two common deadbolt locks are used in most residential facilities. The first is a double-cylinder lock with key entry and exit from both the inside and the outside. The second type (also double cylinder) is operated by a key from the outside and a turn knob from the inside. Consider these points before choosing:

1. If you secure your doors with a double-cylinder lock, remember that you must have a key to open it (when locked) from the inside. This could create a fire hazard in the event of an emergency, so be sure the key is left in place when the house is occupied. Some deadbolt double-cylinder locks have a turn knob/key which, when inserted, acts as a turn knob, but can be removed.

2. During a burglary, a criminal might break through a door, or a window next to the door, to reach in and activate a turnknob type deadbolt. With the

double-cylinder lock (which has no turnknob), this act would be futile. When you have a double-cylinder deadbolt (minus the turnknob), the burglar would not be able to make a fast exit with large objects because the doors would be secure. If your door or adjacent window provides access to locking devices, replace the glass with break-resistant materials that look like glass and resist cutting. Metal grillwork is also very effective here.

Each door to your home should have a one-way peephole or wide-angle viewer (Figure 3-3). Window viewers or small sliding viewers provide you with a fair amount of security when observing and talking to a stranger or delivery man, but even these should be equipped with some form of slide lock or metal grillwork. When possible, install an intercom system, which is the safest form of communication with a visitor. At a minimum, each door should have a slide chain and latch firmly secured to the door and door frame. This slide chain allows you to open the door enough to sign for mail or talk with visitors. Evaluate the security and effectiveness of all door hardware, and apply the necessary safeguards.

Figure 3-3

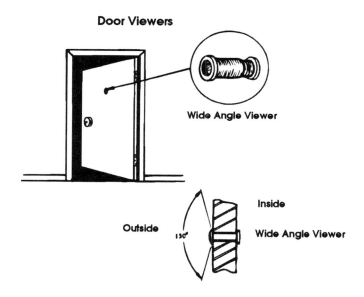

Door Viewers

Wide Angle Viewer

Outside

Inside

Wide Angle Viewer

Double Doors

When securing double doors, be sure that the stationary door is properly equipped with bolts at top and bottom. (Figure 3-4) The operational or opening door should have a deadbolt lock feature as previously discussed.

Figure 3-4

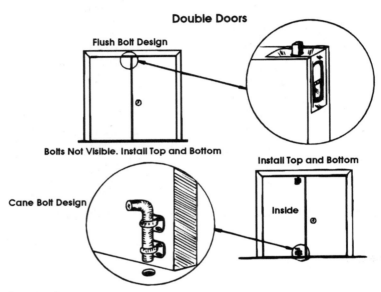

Window Locks

Most windows are easily opened from the outside when not secured with the proper locking devices. When possible, protect all windows with metal grillwork or bars. This is especially important for basement and ground-floor windows. In addition, unbreakable glass or a break-resistant glass substitute can be used to replace or reinforce existing glass. Each individual window should have its own locking mechanism. Use key locks if possible. They mean extra security if the criminal breaks the glass and tries to open a window. But, as with a door, if the frame is old and the wood is rotting, it should be replaced. In addition to existing locks, a simple, effective way to secure double-hung sash windows is to drill a slanted hole through the front (inside) sash, halfway into the rear (outer sash, and insert a metal pin or nail (Figure 3-5).

Figure 3-5

Double Hung Sash Windows

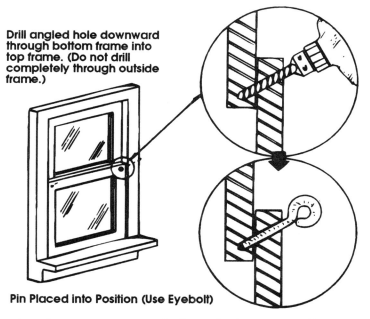

Drill angled hole downward through bottom frame into top frame. (Do not drill completely through outside frame.)

Pin Placed into Position (Use Eyebolt)

Another common window lock, especially on older homes, is the lever latch design or casement-window type (Figure 3-6). This type of latch lock is used on metal frame windows and is opened laterally by hand or by crank. It is very easy to push a coat hanger through a worn window frame to push the lever handle free. In most cases, the burglar will simply break the glass, and reach in and open the latch or operate the crank. To prevent this, remove the cranks and keep them nearby for emergencies, or drill a ¼-inch pin that slides freely in and out of the hole, and cut the ends off flush. Paint the end of the pins so as not to identify their location. If a burglar tries to open the handle, he will run into trouble, and since time is of the essence, he may give up. It's important that all household members be able to remove the pin by pushing it out, or by using a magnet, especially in the event of a fire.

Louvered glass windows are difficult to secure because the individual panes are relatively easy to remove, but you can provide the following safeguards to gain added security (Figure 3-7).

Figure 3-6

Casement Window Latch

1/4 inch hole drilled. Pin prevents latch from opening. Pin should be installed flush with latch on either side.

Figure 3-7

Louvered Window

- Glue each window pane and the clips that hold them in the frame. This will slow the removal process of the windows.

- If clips are aluminum (as most are), purchase steel replacement clips. These are more difficult for the burglar to bend, so it's harder for him to remove the glass.

- Apply window grills, grates, or bars. Remember to consider hazards that exist in case of an emergency. Be sure to install quick releases for these guards, or plan to use an alternate exit.

Closely examine each window on your property to determine how effective the existing lock is. If it does not have a lock, determine the specific type needed and install it immediately. If necessary, check with a security consultant or your local police for suggestions.

Don't forget — window air-conditioning units can be easily pushed in or pulled out of their mounts. To prevent this, make sure they are securely attached.

Sliding Doors/Windows

If your home has sliding doors, you need to be able to secure them effectively. Because most of these doors can be easily pried open, it is important to use a steel rod (commonly called a Charlie Bar) or a length of wood in the door track to keep the door from sliding open.

Most sliding doors also can be lifted off their tracks. To counter this tactic, place one or more screws into the upper track to provide enough clearance so that the door will slide open, yet cannot be lifted off its tracks. Also, you can drill a diagonal slot down through the top frame into the door and insert a nail or metal pin to keep the door from being opened (Figure 3-8).

You can buy and install locks for your sliding doors (Figure 3-9) and windows. Key locks provide excellent protection, but remember to place the key nearby for emergencies.

Figure 3-8

Sliding Glass (Patio) Door

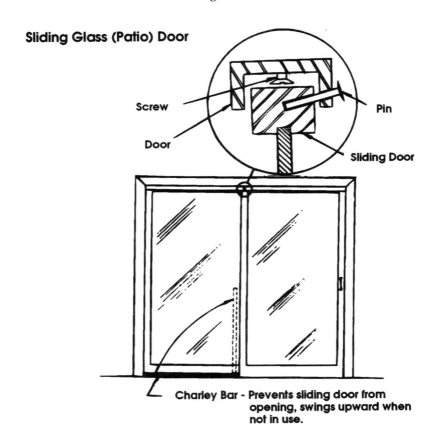

Screw

Door

Pin

Sliding Door

Charley Bar - Prevents sliding door from opening, swings upward when not in use.

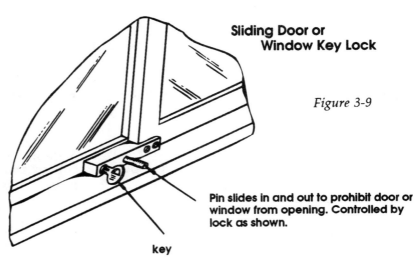

Sliding Door or Window Key Lock

Figure 3-9

Pin slides in and out to prohibit door or window from opening. Controlled by lock as shown.

key

Alternative Window Protection

An additional option available for protecting basement and first-story windows without adding metal grillwork or bars is to plant prickly bushes around all windows. This keeps out the professional who does not want to take the chance of leaving any evidence such as clothing fibers, blood, or skin samples behind. It will also thwart the punk, who doesn't want to get pricked by thorns. The amateur would rather smash the window, thereby alerting neighbors and residents of the break-in.

Padlocks

Outdoor sheds, garage doors, etc., are usually secured with padlocks. If you decide to use one, remember that it, along with a cheap hasp, can be pried or cut off quickly. A padlock should only be used as a deterrent. Always insure that the hasps are strong, secured with bolts, and mounted on a metal plate, and that the bolts are hidden when the lock is applied (Figure 3-10). Look for a padlock that retains its key when open, to help remind you to lock the padlock before you leave (Figure 3-11).

Figure 3-10

Hasp

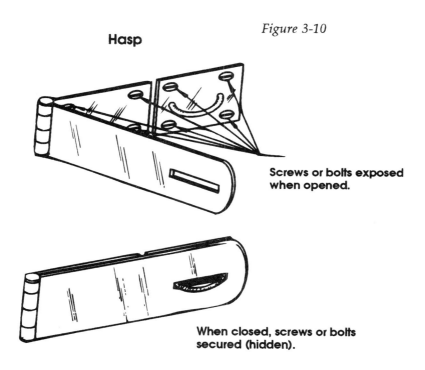

Screws or bolts exposed when opened.

When closed, screws or bolts secured (hidden).

Figure 3-11

Padlocks

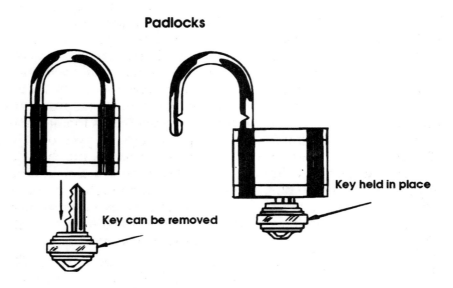

Key held in place

Key can be removed

Miscellaneous Openings.

Even though you have evaluated and secured your doors and windows, a criminal can still gain entrance through cellar doors, crawl spaces under your floors, and air-conditioning and heating system vents and ducts. Secure them appropriately.

One last item: Any time you move into a new home or apartment, chances are that there are other keys floating around which will operate your locks. Consider changing locks or contact a local locksmith to re-key or repin your existing lock system. This can be relatively inexpensive, and may prevent the future loss of valuables.

Alarm Systems

When you buy an alarm system, several things should be considered prior to installation. Do you need to secure a residential area or a commercial area? Exactly what is the value of the property and merchandise you wish to protect? Once you have answered these questions, you can more effectively choose a system that's right for you. The alarm systems available today can perform just about any security function. Make sure you understand the degree of protection you need, then look for the system that will afford you this protection. If you own a $250,000 home, it doesn't make much sense to purchase a system for $100 that will provide $1000 worth of protection. The opposite is also true. Why place a $3,000 alarm system on your $25,000 home and property when a $1,000 system would be just as effective? It's the old story — don't put a $50 lock on a $2 hasp. The system is only as strong as its weakest link.

With such a wide range of systems to choose from, you should have no trouble finding one that both meets your needs and fits your budget. If you require a special, unique system, there are experts who can design, build, and install it for you. I strongly recommend that you shop around until you find the system best for you. It's quite possible that you don't really need an alarm system, even though it is always a plus for added security. Consider all the facts first. Maybe you simply need to improve your existing security and lighting hardware. Adding a lock here, or a light there, will greatly increase your overall security, sometimes much more effectively than alarms. After all, an alarm signals only when an intruder is attempting to enter, or after he is already inside. If the property is secured in the first place, the criminal may not be able to enter at all.

It is next to impossible to discuss all currently available systems here, but to introduce you to the basics involved, let's briefly look at what constitutes an alarm system and how these systems can be employed.

To begin with, all alarm systems contain *sensors*, whose function is to detect and report disturbances caused by a possible intruder. A majority of sensors are of electronic, micro-wave, photoelectric, motion/vibration, audio, or radar design. Most operate by breaking or disturbing an existing electrical current or completing a current. Once an intruder is detected,

the sensor signals the adjoining control panel of the unauthorized entry.

The *control panel unit* is the brains of the alarm system.
Its job is to receive the sensor signal and trigger a local or
central station alarm.

The *alarm* is the device that alerts the operator or
monitor to the presence of an intruder. Bells, sirens, horns, etc.,
are designed to both alert the resident to an unauthorized entry
and scare off the intruder. Lights flashing on and off provide a
visual alarm system to silently notify residents, police or
security personnel, of the entry attempt.

Many sophisticated systems also automatically turn on
lighting systems upon alarm, turn on water sprinkler systems
upon activation of heat sensors, turn off air-condition-
ing/freezer systems upon activation of a temperature drop, or
turn off heating systems upon a temperature rise.

There are three basic systems of alarm response.

1. **Local Alarm**: This system is designed to alert and
    warn personnel within a designated area. The
    alarm can be located on the inside of a building,
    the outside of a building, or a perimeter wall. This
    response system would be recommended for a
    location that is some distance from local police or
    security guards — a farm barn, for example. It will
    generally frighten away both unwanted animals
    and unwanted trespassers.

2. **Central or Remote Stations**: Central or remote
    stations receive the alarm and dispatch police or
    security personnel to investigate. Response time is
    critical, so there are usually officers standing by to
    respond immediately. These systems are used in
    banks, retail stores, etc.

3. **Proprietary**: This system is designed to receive the
    alarm on the secured site, and is handled within
    the protected location by an established security
    force. It is used by large warehouses and apart-
    ment complexes to provide security to property
    and residents.

Alarm systems are either powered by battery (wireless) or by a power source that utilizes wiring (plug-in/generator type), with battery back-up if the main power source is cut. As a rule, your system should include a fire sensing device, and a way to gauge how the system is operating (i.e., poor, weak, dead).

Most alarms are placed at either the perimeter of the area to be protected or within the area itself. Perimeter alarms are used on gates, fences, doors, windows, and other related entrances. They include, but are not limited to, electro-mechanical (circuit design), contact magnetic detectors, glass systems, and electrical switches that are recessed into doors, gates, and windows, and are activated when released.

Interior alarms are set up to detect sound and motion within an established area. They can be motion detection devices (ultrasonic, sonic, and microwave), vibration and seismic (affected by local disturbance), photoelectric cells (usually infrared type) that establish a beam of non-visible light between two designated points, and audio or acoustic alarm systems that can pick up the sound of a pin dropping.

Costs

Local alarm systems can be purchased for anywhere between $10 and $2,000. You could probably build one yourself if you are electrically inclined; but if you do, be sure that it functions properly if you want to save a lot of headaches and frustration later.

Central or remote systems can be installed for $100 to $3,000, depending on your needs. Once installed, there is usually a monthly monitoring fee that can range from $25 to $75. It's best to have experts determine your exact needs, but whichever system you purchase, make sure that it is Underwriters' Laboratories-approved! If you do decide to install an alarm system, check with your insurance company for discount rates.

Proprietary system expenses vary widely, depending on the cost of employing an established local guard force.

Alarm Systems - If You Have One, Use It!

If you decide to install an alarm system in your home or business, use it. Many people go to the expense of getting alarms for property but, after a month or so, the novelty seems to wear off and they cease using the alarm on a regular basis. Still others arm their alarm only when they are away from their homes. We know that a large amount of crime is committed when the home owner is present, even during the day. Unfortunately, many people feel they don't need their alarm when someone is home. Fortunately, most alarm systems today will allow you to alarm different rooms and access points independently, giving you a ring of protection while you travel from one room to another. So, as a minimum, be sure to activate your system to monitor the perimeter and any other area that is not inhabited by a family member.

Your home security program will be only as strong as your weakest link. In most homes, the weak link is the juvenile. It is vital to stress to your children how to properly and consistently use the alarm system, to include use of existing locking and lighting systems as well.

Safes or Fire-Resistant Steel Boxes

Every home and commercial business should have a security safe to protect such highly valuable items as jewels, stocks and bonds, and large sums of cash. There are many different safes on the market today designed to resist forceful entrance. A well-designed safe should have:

- heavy gauge steel walls, top, bottom, and door;
- fire-resistant/retardant material lining its walls; and
- a three-position, dial type, combination locking device.

When contemplating the purchase of a safe, read all accompanying paperwork thoroughly to determine the exact specifications to which the safe is designed, and how secure it is against fire and theft.

The steel used in most safes is designed to resist a certain amount of forceful beating or burning by torches. If a safe or cabinet is not designed to be heat-resistant, you can expect most flammable items inside to burn up if torched. Consider your specific needs, and be sure it's Underwriters'

Laboratories-approved. Many descriptions of containers say they are burglar- and fire-proof. Do not take the description literally. Although safes are resistant to a certain amount of applied force and heat, all safes can be entered, given enough time, and they can also be burned through or melted with extreme heat.

The purpose of safes is to protect valuables from theft and fire, but they are often merely deterrents for the amateur, and a time-consumer for the professional. If he wants to get in, he will, but there are certain measures you can take to improve the security of your safe.

- Chain it to a permanent fixture with a high-security chain and lock.

- Hide home safes in a non-visible locale and tell no one but family members of their existence. Commercial safes should be placed in open, visible, well-lighted areas that can be observed through windows. This prevents burglars from attempting entry unobserved, and allows the safe to be visually checked by passing police or security.

- Maintain strict confidentiality of the combination. The combinations of most purchased safes can be changed by the owner, with no need for a locksmith.

- If it is a commercial safe, use an appropriate alarm system that will alert police or security to a burglary attempt. There are many systems available that are activated by pressure, sound, or heat. Consult an expert on your specific needs.

Security Room

When possible, every home should have a specific room that can provide a high degree of protection to the whole family. "Security rooms" are usually designed to hide residents from intruders, but are never to be used as a refuge against fire. A good example of a home that should have a security room is one that is any great distance from the police. If you are building a home, be sure to include a room of this nature. In an older home, closet space can be converted for this purpose. As a last resort, a central room which is equipped with interior locks and a telephone can serve as a security room. All security rooms should include the following characteristics/supplies:

- The door should be solid hardwood, preferably steel, and should be kept secured at all times to prevent children from locking themselves in.
- The door and door frame should be reinforced.
- An interior lock should be added.
- The outside of the door should not identify the room, if at all possible.
- There should be a light switch to control external lights.
- The room should have adequate internal lighting.
- The telephone's ringer should be tuned down, or removed and replaced with a light. Emergency numbers should be posted.
- Food, water, blankets, first aid and medical supplies, any special medication unique to family members, flashlight and portable radio/TV with batteries, electric socket to provide electricity, and sanitary supplies should be on hand. These could include a weapon, if desired.
- The room should have adequate ventilation.
- An escape door should be provided, if possible.

Remember that you may have to remain in the room for up to one or two days, so maintain adequate supplies. Check the room and supplies for effectiveness periodically, and schedule test runs for family members. It is important never to discuss the existence of a security room with anyone except immediate family members.

Family Security Procedures

Education begins in the home. You and your family should seriously study each other's lifestyles, be it work or school, and point out potential dangers. Everyone should listen and participate. By getting everyone involved, you can get a fairly good idea of the areas of concern facing your family.

Hold meetings to discuss any new ideas, thereby emphasizing the importance of prevention. Strive to develop an attitude of prevention.

As soon as they are old enough to understand, children should be taught:

- Never to talk with strangers.
- Never accept gifts from strangers.
- Never get into a stranger's car.
- Report strangers or suspicious activity to their parents, babysitter, and police immediately.
- Always play in pairs.
- Never open the door without a parent's permission.
- Never hitchhike.
- Always inform their parents where they will be, for how long, and with whom.

The Telephone

The easiest way to gain information not otherwise available is by using the telephone. Anyone who combines a little tact, courtesy, and charm with bits and pieces of previously gathered facts (to make the caller sound legitimate) can usually persuade an individual to provide the requested information. For this reason, it is of the utmost importance to train all family members, secretaries, maids, babysitters, etc., on how and what to say over the phone.

To start with, it might not be a bad idea to request an unlisted telephone number. You can provide your number to your friends and relatives, while keeping the random caller off the line. If a call is important, there are emergency methods of locating you through the operator. Provide employers, schools, hospitals, etc., with your number when necessary. Request a one-party line.

- Never provide your name or phone number to a person calling whom you think has the wrong number. Ask him what number he wants, and politely say, "Sorry, this is not that number." If the caller persists, hang up immediately.

- Never answer questions over the phone asked by strangers, especially those who request personal information, such as what bank you deal with, how much money you have in your savings, or your account numbers.

- Beware of a caller identifying himself as an employee of your bank, stating that they have had a computer breakdown and need some pertinent information on your checking/savings accounts. In a case like this, always request the caller's name and number and tell him you will return his call. Do not use the number that the caller has provided, but look up the number of your bank in your phone directory, and use that one if they are indeed different. Ask to speak to the bank manager or the head teller and explain your situation. If the call was legitimate, they will know of it. If not, notify the police immediately.

- Never discuss over the phone that you are alone.

- Never discuss vacation or time schedules.

- If you are a female living alone, do not list your full name in the phone directory. Use just your first and middle initial with your last name. Many crank callers pick on women who live alone.

- Never keep your phone off the hook. You never know who is attempting to call you in case of an emergency.

- Do not be tricked into providing information to someone saying, "Congratulations, you have just won a new car, television set, or microwave oven! Please confirm for us your phone number, address, etc." Always ask them to identify themselves and whom they represent, and make sure you have entered the contest that you have just won. Most sponsors of contests notify their winners by mail, so be very careful.

- Do not answer telephone survey questions. Request the caller to send you a questionnaire by mail.
- Never allow children to answer the telephone unless supervised by an adult.
- Children should be taught how to dial the police and fire department. It is also good for them to know their own phone number including area code. Test them.
- Do not tie up the telephone for lengthy periods of time. If you expect important calls, consider contacting your phone company to add the "call waiting" feature. This will insure that you won't miss an emergency call.
- Report trouble with your phone immediately.
- If a telephone repairman arrives, check to see if you can see his truck or van. Does he have his tools? Can he identify himself? Call the phone company when possible to confirm his story.

Obscene Phone Calls

- Hang up immediately on obscene phone callers. Do not engage in conversation or shouting matches. This is what they want.
- Report all crank or obscene phone calls to the police and the telephone company. After a while, if enough complaints stack up, they may decide to attempt to "trap" the caller.
- If you receive a "heavy breather" or obscene caller, hang up. If he continues, blow a loud shrieking, high pitched whistle or air horn into the phone, which should get your message across.
- If he continues, tell him the police have been notified and are monitoring the line.
- If necessary, change your phone number.

Another option is a telephone answering machine. Most machines will allow you to monitor all incoming calls. Some answering machines have an optional "memo record" feature, which allows you to record the conversation between you and the caller. A recorded message from, or conversation with, a suspected obscene caller can be turned over to the police for their appropriate use.

Already in existence in some areas is a telephone feature which will allow only specified calls to be received. Still another feature will allow you to see the name and/or number of the person calling, giving you the choice to accept or deny the call.

Strangers at your Door

Never, under any circumstances, allow a stranger access to your house. Always determine what he wants, and confirm his story. A large number of rapes and robberies begin with a courteous smile and a polite hello. Many times, a criminal "cases" his potential target by gaining entrance under false pretenses.

Keep the Criminal Outside

- Never allow a stranger into your home. If he asks to use the phone to call a tow truck, inform him you will make the call for him.

- Never allow children to answer the door, especially if they are left alone. As a minimum, teach them to call a neighbor first, informing them of their visitor.

- Never admit maintenance personnel without first confirming who they are. These few moments will not ruin the schedule. If you never called them, get the name, full identification, vehicle description, and license number. Then call the business to confirm why they are there. If no adequate answer is given, call the police.

- Never leave a stranger alone with your children or alone in any room.

- Inform servants not to let a stranger in until identification is confirmed.
- Always observe visitors through a peephole or window.
- Never open the door to strangers without using the safety chain, and hold one foot securely against the base of the door.
- Report all suspicious activity and strange vehicles to police immediately.
- Ask sales people to leave brochures in the mail box or outside the door.

Reporting a Crime or Suspicious Activity

Many crimes could be stopped if people would just pick up the phone and call the police. It's not a requirement to provide your name, if you feel uncomfortable about it. The important thing is to report the crime.

Be Aware of Suspicious Behavior

Take note of any activity not considered usual, such as:
- A stranger closely observing a home or car.
- Someone attempting to enter a home or car using force, or having difficulty in obtaining entrance.
- Anyone standing in or around bushes or behind objects, attempting to conceal himself.
- Someone running from a home.
- Someone screaming.
- A moving van with workers loading furniture from a home when you doubt that the residents are present or that they intend to move.
- A stranger talking with or offering candy or rides to children.
- Someone who dresses and acts in ways that are inappropriate to the neighborhood or the weather.
- A stranger parked in a car closely observing people and residences.

- Someone peeking in windows
- A vehicle that repeatedly drives slowly through your neighborhood.
- Someone who knocks on the front door or rings the door bell, and then goes around to the rear of the house.
- An abandoned vehicle.

Obtain a Good Description

Providing the police with an accurate description of a stranger or criminal can, in many cases, be the key to a quick and effective arrest. Always observe the situation and record the following:

- Sex of the individual.
- Height.
- Weight.
- Race.
- Clothes — color, style, accessories (hat, jewelry, etc.), type of footwear.
- Hair color, length, style, including facial hair.
- Eye color, shape; eyeglasses.
- Physical build.
- Physical deformities.
- Verbal/speech patterns.
- Any conversation or names you overhear.

Vehicles

- License number, state.
- Type of vehicle (car, truck, motorcycle, van, etc.).
- Color.
- Make, model and year.
- Two-door or four-door.
- Visible damage.

- Extras (e.g., telephone or CB antenna, ski rack).
- Time and direction of travel.
- How many occupants.

How To Report A Crime

Always call the police immediately upon suspecting suspicious activity. It's better to be a little embarrassed if nothing is wrong than to let a criminal escape. Remember:

- Time is very important. Report the crime immediately.
- Always remain calm and collected.
- Provide the police with your name, address, and phone number.
- Provide the police with the address of the suspicious activity.
- Tell the police what the suspicious activity is.
- Provide the police a complete description of the suspect and of any vehicle involved.

What To Do When Surprised by an Intruder

Everyone has at some time worried about the possibility that they or a member of their family will be home when a criminal decides to force his way in. What should a person do in this kind of situation?

When an intruder demands your money and jewelry, always obey him. Any struggle or resistance on your part may get you or another family member hurt. As in all threatening situations, resistance should be used only as a last resort. Remain calm, and allow the burglar to escape uncontested. Above all, never attempt to chase after him. Call the police and provide an accurate report of the incident and description of the criminal.

Next, determine where and how the intruder managed to enter without being heard or seen, and take whatever measures are necessary to prevent another unexpected visit. If your home had been properly secured, with adequate locks and lighting, most intruders would not have been able to forcefully enter without being heard. Unfortunately, many times the burglar simply walks through an unlocked back door or crawls through an open window.

Let's assume now that you have taken every precautionary measure possible to ward off an intruder, and one still tries to force his way in. What now? Several actions can be taken, provided each action is safe, practical, and based on common sense.

To start with, let's say that one night you suspect that someone is attempting to force open your back door. A quick look through the back window confirms your suspicions. First, call the police, then turn on every light possible to try to frighten him off. Gather up family members and exit through the front door, running to a neighbor for help. If for some reason you cannot escape immediately and safely, retreat to your security room if you have one.

If your only other alternative is to sit tight and wait for help, find a spot in your house that offers concealment while, if possible, providing observation of the area the intruder is trying to enter. Grab a weapon like a ball bat, golf club, fireplace poker, or knife, and yell a warning to the burglar. Let him know that you have called the police (even if for some reason you were unable to do so), and inform him you have a weapon and will use it if he continues. You might even consider barking ferociously like a killer dog. Sounds silly, but anything that will cause the intruder to have second thoughts is worth the effort.

Actually, any intelligent criminal (any criminal with average intelligence), is going to run as soon as you hit the lights. If the intruder's activity appears to stop, continue to expect the unexpected. He could be waiting for you to open a door or window to check out the situation, which will make it easier for him to attack. Remain alert and calm, and still be sure to call the police to report the incident. They should place a patrol in the area to watch for further suspicious activity.

Most criminals want to remain unseen and unheard. But what about the one who is under the influence of drugs or alcohol, or possibly mentally disturbed? Since he cannot think rationally, rational actions to scare him off may not work. These criminals are very, very dangerous and will quite possibly attack you because you are in their way. You must avoid them at all costs.

What about the intruder who, fearing nothing, rips the door off its hinges and continues advancing? Now it's either submit totally and hope for mercy, or stand and fight. Given enough time to prepare, and the proper attitude, the home-owner can, in most cases, drop the intruder where he stands. This is accomplished by obtaining a weapon and taking a position affording the advantage of surprise.

If armed with a firearm, shoot a warning shot (if you have enough time) into a solid piece of furniture. This should keep the bullet from penetrating a wall and striking an innocent person. It should convince him to turn and run, but if not, you may have to shoot him. At this time, don't concern yourself with legalities. If the incident happened as described here, the use of deadly force would probably be justified, since you feared bodily harm or death.

If you are armed with a club or knife, your initial attack must be forceful and accurate. Use whatever force is necessary to stop the criminal. Once you overpower the assailant, make sure he is totally unable to retaliate. Tie him up or stand guard over him with a weapon until help arrives. Never render first aid if there is a chance that he may grab you and continue his plans. Do so only when you are 100 percent positive that you can provide aid without endangering yourself or another family member. Remember, this guy is probably desperate and would take whatever measure necessary to overpower you and escape. If possible, call for an ambulance.

Awakened by an Intruder?

What should you do when you wake up and realize an intruder is already prowling around inside your home? Usually the best approach is to stay in bed and pretend to be asleep until you can escape, lock your door, or call the police. It's possible the burglar won't even see you; if he does, chances are he will leave or continue quietly before exiting.

In some cases, if the intruder has other plans (assault or rape), you'd better be prepared either to consent or to resist. You may be better off submitting to all demands. This does not mean you chose to be assaulted, but that you had no other way to insure your safety or the safety of the child in the next room.

If you decide to resist, do so intelligently. Take advantage of the element of surprise, which is on your side. Secure a weapon (knife, club, firearm), possibly concealed under your mattress, and wait to see if he will enter and approach you. Don't make any sudden moves until he is directly over you. It is possible that he may enter your room only to search for valuables, then quietly exit. Any quick act on your part here could prove fatal to you unless you are absolutely sure of success.

If he decides to wake you or physically assault you, he probably will get within arm's reach to check you out. Let him get as close as possible, then let him have it with all you've got until you are sure you are safe. Always remember you are taking the chance that this could backfire on you. He could take any weapon you have away and use it against you. This decision is strictly up to you, based on the circumstances at hand.

It is very important for each family to establish some form of defensive plan against intruders. It is also a good idea to teach household employees and babysitters how to react to this threat.

Listing and Marking Your Valuables

Two important ways to cut your losses in case of theft or fire are to maintain an updated inventory of your property and to mark all valuables with a registration identification number.

By keeping an accurate list of your property (including stocks, bonds, and securities), you will know when something is missing. In case of fire, you can immediately supply your insurance agent with this list. In case of burglary, you can quickly pinpoint the missing items and notify the police immediately. The sooner the theft is reported, the better your chance to regain your property if it is located.

The best way to identify your property is to mark it with a special code (social security number, state abbreviation, driver's license number, etc.). This can be done with an engraving tool or with invisible marking techniques such as the ultraviolet pen, which reveals the marking only when placed under ultraviolet light. Since it's invisible, it prevents the thief from sanding off your identification number.

Your inventory list should include a detailed description of each item, with serial numbers or identification numbers, value of item, when purchased, and, if possible, a copy of the sales receipt (Figure 3-12). It's very important to supply your insurance agent with a complete copy of your inventory list, and to update it periodically. It's also wise to keep an additional copy in a safe deposit box or with a trusted relative. Another safety technique: photographic records of your valuables, especially high-value items like jewelry, coins, art, and antiques.

Whenever a robbery or larceny is committed and reported to the police, any identification on stolen objects is logged into the National Crime Information Center (NCIC) computer. When items are returned or recovered, the computer is searched by using available serial numbers or other recorded identification, and the property can be returned if claimed.

Marked property is frowned upon by burglars because it can quickly be traced. Thus, by applying warning stickers to your doors (back and front) and windows, you can help deter burglary. Most police departments will help you mark your valuables and can also provide warning stickers.

Hiring Household Staff

Anyone who enjoys the same freedoms within a home as the family members (babysitters, maids, butlers), should be completely honest and trustworthy. Unfortunately, the days of unlocked doors and unquestioned friendships are coming to an end. How often do we read about babysitters or housekeepers who assaulted, kidnapped, or killed a child in their care?

It is extremely important to thoroughly evaluate prospective household employees. Expect the same qualities and concerns from the housekeeper as from yourself. If they are uneducated about family protection, teach them. Your family's safety is at stake.

Figure 3-12
Inventory List

Name: _____

Address: _____

City: _____ State: _____ Zip: _____

Phone Number: _____

Insurance Company: _____

Address: _____

Phone Number: _____

Claim Number: _____

Date of Inventory: _____ Updated On: _____

ROOM	ITEM ID/SERIAL #	VALUE	DATE OF PUR.	MISC. DATA

Records of Stocks, Bonds, and Insurance Policies

TYPE OF SECURITY	VALUE AMOUNT	POLICY NUMBER

Every employee should be subject to a police records check, at the very minimum. Anyone who shies away from this request could have something to hide. If they should say, "So I made one mistake; it won't happen again," don't base your family's well-being on whether this person has reformed.

Trust also depends on what type of record a person might have. Although an extensive history of driving violations does not mean this person is irresponsible, arrests for drunk driving would be grounds for disqualifying him or her for a position that requires child care or supervision.

A record that shows a petty theft charge during high school ten years ago, however, does not necessarily mean the applicant should be disqualified. You must use common sense and consider the time period involved. People do grow up and mature. We all have weaknesses, but be sure the weaknesses your employees have cannot harm your family. An example of a household staff profile is found in Figure 3-13.

Additional skills, such as first aid training, CPR, or registered nurse are an obvious plus. Anyone who demonstrates an interest in safety and security should be strongly considered.

Don't feel obligated to hire friends and relatives for these positions. Most people hesitate to express their true feelings to such employees simply because they are friends or relatives. You must be able to establish guidelines and enforce them rigorously.

Babysitters should be mature enough to understand and carry out your instructions completely. They must be able to handle situations that may require difficult decisions, including precautions against burglars. Do not assume they can handle all situations. Question them and run them through a series of practical tests to see what they know and how well they react to pressure.

By all means, forbid the babysitter to have guests, especially a girlfriend or boyfriend. All attention must be given to the job at hand to insure adequate responses to an unexpected emergency. The *first* time orders are disobeyed, fire him or her. That first time could have cost the life of your child.

Figure 3-13
Staff Background Data

Staff Position: _____

Full Name/Alias: _____

Date/Place of Birth: _____

Address: _____

Home Phone: _____

Prior Employment: _____

Address: _____ **Phone:**_____

Former Supervisor: _____

References: _____

Special Qualifications *(First Aid, CPR, Nurse, Bodyguard, etc.)*: _____

_____

Misc. Data: * _____

_____

Local Agency Checks:
☐ **Local Police Results** _____
☐ **Local Court (If necessary)** _____

_____
Signature of Staff Member

_____
Date

*OPTION: *Include statement informing applicant of possible polygraph examination prior to and during employment.*

Emphasis must be on prevention. Maids, butlers, house-keepers, and maintenance personnel must be fully aware of family security procedures and follow them to the letter. Work toward developing a family relationship whenever possible; staff personnel are more aware and responsible when they feel it's more than just a job.

When you are away for a night or longer, always tell the housekeeper or babysitter exactly where you will be. I recommend a bulletin board that displays specific instructions, including your location, phone number, when you intend to return, and any special medicine to be administered to children. Your address should be prominently displayed, so that in case of an emergency it can be relayed properly to authorities (Figure 3-14). Keep a Family Data File (Figure 3-15) on each family member and make it accessible to staff personnel in case of an emergency.

Figure 3-14
For Family Bulletin Board

Family's Name: _____

Address: _____

Phone Number: _____

We are at: _____ **Phone:** _____

We will be back at: _____

In case of emergency contact: _____

At Phone Number: _____

Police: _____ **Fire:** _____

Hospital: _____ **Poison Control:** _____

Doctor's Name/Number: _____

Special Instructions: _____

_____

Figure 3-15

Emergency Information
Family Data File

Name: _____

Date/Place of Birth: _____

Age: _____ Sex: _____ Blood Type: _____

Special Medications: _____

Allergies/Reactions: _____

_____

Special Instructions: _____

_____

Doctor's Name/Number: _____

Religion: _____

NOTE: Complete for each member of the family.

Rural Crime

More than eight million crimes occur each year in rural areas. This is partly because large quantities of farm equipment and other valuable items are inadequately protected, including farm animals that are not properly marked or branded for identification.

Equipment

To help fight crime on the farm, you must establish a program of crime prevention. As essential steps in your program, you should:

- Light all areas of the farm.
- Place locks on storage sheds, feed and grain elevators, gas pumps, and farm tools such as plows, discs, etc. These should be chained to a permanent fixture.

- Never leave large equipment in the fields at night. Lock them in a barn or shed or to a permanent fixture that is well-lighted.

- Use alarm systems, if possible, on all vehicles, or, at a minimum, include a "kill-switch" to keep ignition from starting.

- Inventory and mark all equipment with social security number and state. Place markings in two locations, the first in a visible area. The second should be in a concealed, secret location, so that if the first marking is sanded off or painted over, you can still identify the object. Also take photographs of all your large, more valuable equipment, giving copies to your insurance agent.

Establishing
A Neighborhood
Watch Program

Throughout the United States, and throughout the world, concerned citizens are volunteering their time and effort in the fight against crime in their communities. Some of the best ways to do this are to get involved in a neighborhood watch program, crime stoppers association, church activities, or to develop a crime prevention program for your area with the assistance of your local police. There are many benefits to programs of this nature, but the true goal of a neighborhood watch program is the protection of life and property.

As an organized group, neighborhood watchers have more influence on city hall than just one person. They can pressure city government to close "drug houses" or buildings that provide a safe haven for illegal activity. They can request community improvements that aid in exposing crime, such as better street and park lighting. They can identify those areas that are in need of additional police patrolling, and can assist in identifying the development of gangs and/or gang-related problems.

How to Get Started

An interest in forming a neighborhood watch program can be generated by a citizen, a school, or a civic or church group coordinating with the local police department. Most police departments welcome any organized and controlled assistance they can get.

The community must be educated about the causes and effects of crime, as well as how to plan prevention. Once a sincere interest begins to grow, there should be a meeting (usually organized by the police department) where the neighborhood watch program proposal is discussed and the specific areas of concern identified.

What is Required

The neighborhood watch program's primary function is to observe and report suspicious/illegal activity. The emphasis is on reporting crime, not engaging it. Let common sense be your guide. The community as a whole can provide much better visual observation than any police department no matter how large, simply because there are more citizens than officers.

For the first step, a police representative is usually assigned to assist the neighborhood in establishing its neighborhood watch program. This representative will normally contact key individuals to organize a community meeting. Included in this meeting should be the mayor, councilmen, businessmen, and any other interested citizens of the community. It is best to hold this type of meeting at a location that can handle a large crowd.

During the meeting, the police representative should discuss the proposal, give a crime prevention presentation and/or show a movie about establishing a neighborhood watch program.

Once the major details are discussed and understood, the citizens should identify the specific geographical boundaries to be included in their watch program. They should select a neighborhood watch chairman and individual block captains to supervise the program, and form a watch committee to help guide and oversee the program.

Once the group has been organized, it should formulate organizational by-laws which address such articles as:

- Designation and purpose of the program
- Membership
- Duties of officers
- Rights and privileges
- Methods of elections
- Officers
- Amendments

Monthly meetings (at the town hall or local church) should be scheduled for block captains, always including the police department representative. An annual membership meeting should be held to re-elect new officers and introduce new members.

Be certain to get adequate media coverage to advertise this new program to other interested citizens. This also serves to warn criminals that from then on the citizens will be watching and reporting any suspicious activities or individual(s).

Establish neighborhood watch rosters and charts that clearly identify all the neighborhood boundaries, member names, phone numbers, addresses, etc. Be sure that permission is received prior to distribution of personal information, such as phone numbers, to other members. The neighborhood watch captain, his committee, and police should get a copy of the total breakdown of the neighborhood.

Prepare literature that describes techniques of crime prevention. Design and print up decals and stickers to help advertise your activity.

Establish guidelines on how to observe suspicious activity, how to obtain a good description of an incident, and how to report it to the police. Familiarize each member with surrounding homes, addresses and phone numbers, to aid in speedy reporting of suspicious activity (Figure 4-1). Insist that all activity be written down and kept by the neighborhood watch chairman for future use.

Figure 4-1

Alert Roster
Neighborhood Watchers Reporting Procedures:

Watcher(Emergency) ➡ Police Department ➡ Block Captain
Watcher (Non-Emergency) ➡ Block Captain ➡ Neighborhood
Watch Chairman ➡ Police

When reporting an emergency, notify your local police immediately, then block captain. When reporting a non-emergency, contact your block captain, who contacts the neighborhood watch chairman who should make the appropriate reports for future use.

Neighborhood Watchers should be able to identify each of their neighbors' residences and maintain the appropriate addresses and phone numbers to inform police in the event of an emergency.

Watcher's Name:_____

Address: _____ Phone Number: _____

Police Phone Number: _____ Fire Phone Number: _____

Hospital/Rescue Phone Number: _____

Block Captain's Name: _____

Address: _____ Phone Number: _____
NOTE: Block Captain should have Watch Chairman listed on his/her chart.

Activity Spotted: _____

Location: _____ Date: _____ Time: _____

Descriptions of Personal/Vehicles:_____

_____

Your neighborhood watch program should become involved in establishing crime prevention techniques and performing security surveys. Other valuable programs can also be implemented, such as:

- The inventory and marking of valuables to be recorded and placed in a secure file at the police department.
- Assistance for senior citizens.
- Child safety and identification programs.
- Courses in defensive tactics.
- Establishing a crime prevention month.
- Establishing a volunteer program designed to allow authorized civilians to assist the local police in crime prevention.

It's important for each community to use its resources to the fullest. Tackle one or two specific crime problems at a time, and watch the program grow in size and accomplishments. Don't try to attack every possible problem in the community at the same time, or you will find the committees overburdened and spread too thin to be of any real assistance.

Ingredients of a Strong Program

1. Be sure all members are residents of the neighborhood. It would, to say the least, be counter-productive for crooks to join your organization!
2. Try not to schedule too much work or too many meetings for volunteers. Remember, they have their families to take care of first.
3. Take time to become established and operational.
4. Include all areas of crime prevention.
5. Don't overstep bounds and interfere with other's rights by believing you are now a police representative and have authority to enforce laws. You will only create hard feelings among the community and give the neighborhood watch program a bad name.

A Pooch for Protection

I f a little additional security and companionship is desired, consider getting a pooch for protection. Whether you acquire a professionally trained guard dog or find a loveable mutt at the pound, dogs can effectively deter crime.

For many years dogs have been used to guard property and lives, to search out contraband, to track down criminals and lost children, and to guide the blind. The services a dog can provide seem endless, not to mention the love and loyalty they show for their owners.

Although not all pets are going to jump between you and a potential mugger, an obedient canine can provide you with an invaluable psychological advantage over a criminal. Many dogs have been known to give their lives for their masters. Few people will take the chance of entering your property or attacking your person when it's obvious a dog is present.

Short, tall, fat, or skinny, a dog can scare the daylights out of just about anyone not familiar with its abilities. A dog in the home or roving on the property will, in most cases, keep a criminal away. Since time and concealment are the most important factors to a thief, if they are confronted with a barking dog or find themselves staring at a dog between them and their target, they will probably think twice, and seek a more secluded, less noisy, and "safer" home to enter. If, while a criminal attempts to break into a residence, he sees or hears a dog yapping away inside, his intentions may change. A barking dog is a roving alarm system. Why risk it? As long as this is the philosophy of the criminal, the dog, professionally trained or not, will remain invaluable!

Do you need a professionally trained guard or attack dog, or will the average house pet be sufficient? Experts in this field have varied opinions regarding trained guard dogs.

Professional guard or attack dogs are generally trained by experts in this field, but some authorities say you can train your own dog under the supervision of an expert trainer.

Guard and attack dogs are trained primarily to react very aggressively to any and all situations pertaining to their duties. Their main goal is to guard, deter, or engage an intruder. Because they are trained to react so aggressively, these dogs should not be taken home as family pets. Most professional dogs of this nature are kept in pens, awaiting their tour of duty, and do not reside with the average family.

Some experts do say that a professional guard or attack dog can leave its job and then be taken home among the family, without fear of injury to children or adults.

Professional dogs are trained to obey specific commands. These commands can be conveyed verbally, or with hand movements, or by using both methods, depending on training. These dogs are usually obedient to only one master. What about the family member who startles or accidentally signals the dog to attack? Or is the possibility that this would happen very small because such animals obey only their master's commands?

These comments raise questions in many minds. "If professional trainers disagree, should I risk my family's safety by exposing them to a professional guard/attack dog as a pet?" I am neither in favor of nor against bringing a guard dog, professionally trained or otherwise, into your home. My interest is only to *alert* you to the possible dangers involved when exposed to any animal trained to be aggressive.

After all, there have been occasions when so-called family pets have killed their owners, so to condemn professional dogs is hardly fair. I have personally worked with professional guard and attack dogs and felt comfortable petting and playing with them. I have also worked with those who would just as soon take your arm off as look at you.

It all boils down to how well the animal is trained, what conditions it is exposed to, and how much affection is provided. Be aware that there are many so-called professional trainers of dogs who are phonies. Because there is a lot of money to be made by training and selling professional guard and attack dogs, the business attracts many unscrupulous people out to make a fast buck.

If you are seriously considering purchasing a professionally-trained dog for security reasons, then snoop around and get one that's fully qualified. Take the time to ask other dog owners which trainers they would recommend, and which ones you should avoid. Check your phone directory for ones near you, but visit more than one to be safe. Ask yourself, "How long has this trainer been around? Has anybody heard of him, or purchased one of his animals? What sort of track record do the trainer and his dogs have?" Check with your local kennel association, protective league, dog pound, and/or police.

Once you visit a trainer, have him thoroughly run the dog through his commands. It is important that the trainer can effectively control the dog. Be sure to test how quickly the animal obeys the command to cease its attack! It's just as important that he be able to respond to your commands! Make sure the animal has its required shots and is healthy. Any dog that shows signs of beatings, or appears sickly, may have been mistreated, and is a time bomb.

After you purchase your dog, or even if you rent one from an owner to patrol your business, remember you are responsible and liable for its actions. Proper barriers must be constructed and warning signs posted to keep the animal from accidentally escaping and attacking an innocent victim. Since this dog's primary role is to protect, and he is capable of aggressiveness, be sure to provide the necessary safeguards to prevent an accidental injury.

Professional guard and attack dogs have been and will continue to be irreplaceable. Their actions have protected an indeterminable amount of property, but, most importantly, they have guarded and saved lives.

If you decide that this is the protection you need, then feel comfortable in the knowledge that these animals perform, probably in most cases, with more courage and instinct than a human.

Now let's talk about the average house dog found across the country. Does he have to be big, or bark ferociously? No, he doesn't. With the exception of the determined professional, the mere presence of a dog in most cases will keep a person from entering your residence. (If the professional intends to break in, he will be prepared. He will either drug your dog, maneuver his attention elsewhere, or possibly even shoot him.)

Is There a "Best" Breed?

For a family, the "best" dog will be the one that provides the most love and affection. Of course, size has advantages and disadvantages. If you live in a small apartment, a large German Shepherd would be impractical, but a tiny Chihuahua can provide affection and bark its little head off at the first indication of an intruder. If you live on a large ranch or farm, then several midsize to large dogs may be your answer. They have room to run and can effectively deter trespassers over a large territory.

I would not give up one dog for another because he doesn't seem to be the courageous protector you had hoped. All dogs develop a sense of loyalty, and establish their boundaries or domain. When tested, they will at least appear to stand their ground. Remember, the stranger does not know what actions your dog will take. When approached by a suspicious-looking stranger, just attach a leash to your pet (even if you know that Spot is not going anywhere and he just stares at you in confusion), and warn the intruder to depart. If necessary, act like you are about to unleash a terrible killer upon him. Once he leaves, you both can go back inside and have a good laugh and a milkbone.

How Do Dogs React?

As a rule, when a dog is approached, he will react in one of the following ways:

1. He will run up to you, wag his tail, sniff the various scents on your clothes, and try to jump all over you, wanting you to pet him. A pushover, this dog will make friends with everyone and anyone.

2. He will stand his ground, barking, or remain silent. This is the one that you cannot be sure of. He could attack or run away.

3. At the first sign of company, he will run and hide with his tail between his legs, usually tossing a bark or two at you from behind the couch or from behind the legs of his owner. He is not really a direct physical threat — his bark really is worse than his bite!

4. He will immediately spring to meet you — growling, snarling, and possibly snapping, daring you to move another inch. Whatever you do, don't turn and run. Freeze and wait for help. This one is likely to draw blood.

Recognizing Threats In the Work Environment

T he buses were running late that morning — six inches of new snow had fallen the night before. Sarah was worried that she would be late for a meeting. She opted for the warmer, drier, faster subway. In her hurry, she didn't notice the teenager sneaking up on her. She stared in amazement as he ran off with her shoulder bag into the rush-hour traffic.

Our daily ritual of going to work can become so routine that we find ourselves taking for granted ordinary actions like walking to the car or waiting for a bus. With our thoughts elsewhere, we often forget, for example, to check the inside of the car before we get in. This simple but very important act might someday save your life. So, as in the chapter on home environments, we must carefully and thoroughly examine the areas of danger that may threaten us when we leave home and venture out into the "jungle."

Leaving Home

Before you leave home, be sure that you have locked all your doors and windows. Make sure all appliances (stove, iron, coffee maker) are turned off or unplugged to prevent accidents.

Double-check the front door on the way out, and by all means leave a light on if you intend to return home after nightfall.

Personal Transportation

The threat of an attack is particularly great for individuals who live in apartments or homes that require parking in public lots or on the street. If possible, lock your vehicle inside a secure garage. If you must park outside or in an indoor parking lot, opt for a spot that is not secluded.

If you live in an apartment complex with indoor public parking, I suggest you get together with the other tenants and request proper lighting and the installation of an alarm system. If you are really persuasive, the landlord may hire a guard to watch the premises. Unfortunately, it may take a crime or series of crimes before this happens.

At the minimum, create a buddy system, where two of you meet at a designated time and proceed to your cars together. It's harder to rendezvous for a return trip, so try to leave during daylight hours, or get a friend to accompany you if you must leave later. You may be able to call ahead before leaving work and have a friend or relative meet you. When possible, carpool with members of your apartment complex, which is a very economical and safe way to travel.

Before getting in a vehicle, always take a good look inside to be sure no one is there. If the doors that you locked are unlocked, do not get inside. Return to your residence and call police, or at least ask a friend to check it out with you.

Once safely inside your vehicle, always lock your doors and roll windows up. Keep a half-tank of fuel in the vehicle for safety's sake. In addition, every vehicle should carry these items:

- First-aid kit
- Blankets
- Spare tire (check periodically for condition)
- Tire-changing tools
- Fire extinguisher
- Flares or reflectors
- White flag or rag

- Appropriate repair tools
- If possible, install a telephone or Citizens Band radio in your vehicle for emergencies

If your car breaks down along the way to work, always pull off the road, out of the path of oncoming traffic. Pull into a driveway or business parking lot, if possible, to perform repairs. If you're along the road in an unfamiliar area and have no help immediately available, you should:

- Open the hood and raise it all the way.
- At night, place flares or reflectors approximately 40 feet in front of and behind the vehicle.
- Tie a white flag on the door of the driver's side or the car's radio or CB antenna.
- Remain in the vehicle with the doors locked
- Keep the vehicle in park and engine off, to prevent the possibility of carbon monoxide poisoning. Remember — carbon monoxide is not always identifiable by its smell. It usually enters your system undetected, causing unconsciousness, then death.
- If changing a tire, always block the front tires when jacking up the rear, and block the rear tires and apply the emergency brake when jacking up the front. Don't accidentally lock your keys in the trunk or inside the car or you will be in even worse shape.
- If another motorist stops to help, you must judge whether to accept it or not. It is usually recommended that you roll your window down, ask the motorist to call for a service truck or family member, or wait for a police car to arrive. They can request help for you.
- Never pick up hitchhikers.

If, while you are driving to work, another driver begins to harass you with his vehicle, attempts to get you to stop, or tries to force you off the road, keep driving until you can find help. Never stop to argue with a person like this. Write down their license number and a description of the vehicle and driver, then notify the police.

Public Transportation

Every day, thousands rely on the public transportation system to get them to and from work. Although most public systems provide police or security services, there are many that do not. Even where police security services are available, they are usually spread out over a large area, making immediate response to an illegal activity difficult or impossible. The best thing you can do for protection is to be aware of the people and the activities around you.

On buses, you are fairly safe since there usually are many riders. When waiting for a bus, remain alert for potential purse snatchers or muggers. Stay with the general crowd and secure all packages tightly. *Never* leave a bag or package unattended. Do not exit a bus in an unfamiliar area. If you are lost, ask the driver for help or remain on the bus until it arrives in a familiar locale or returns to its terminal.

Seat yourself as close to the front as possible, and watch for pickpockets. On a crowded bus, a pickpocket can have a field day with unsuspecting riders. Keep all bags and briefcases in plain sight — on your lap if at all possible. As you get off the bus, be alert for purse-snatchers and muggers waiting to nab you as you step down.

In taxis, make sure you have flagged down a legitimate taxi service. Unfamiliar or suspicious-looking vehicles should never be entered. Once inside, make sure the usual items found inside (meter, maps, charts, change box) are present, or get out immediately. Provide clear instructions, and if the driver deviates from them, create an excuse to stop. Get out, and notify police and taxi headquarters. Make sure to obtain the license number, taxi number, and description of the vehicle and driver. (Think how easy it would be to fix up a car to look like a local taxi and abduct or rob potential customers!)

Subways and trains have underground threats. Plan accordingly. Know where the driver and security guards are located and move to that locale if possible. When in doubt, exit the train. Never stay in an area that could be dangerous, especially an unlighted car that's empty.

When traveling by air, always comply with all rules and regulations of the carrier. Plan your travel arrangements completely, and always confirm scheduled flights. Leave a copy of your itinerary with someone. Lock all baggage and mark all pieces with your complete address and phone number. Remove flight tags from previous trips to prevent an accidental misrouting of your luggage. I recommend that you always keep hand-carried items with you while waiting for your flight, and not lock them in airport lockers. Lockers are generally easily broken into, and sometimes more than one key exists to open them. If children are accompanying you, never allow them out of your sight.

Once you arrive at your destination by personal or public means, if you are parking a vehicle, always park in a visible, well lighted location, with windows up and keys in your possession before locking the doors. Walk with others when possible, especially at night, with your keys firmly in your hand to help defend against a possible mugger.

If you must park underground or in a secluded parking lot, try not to be alone. These lots are very dangerous locations, so obtain an escort if at all possible, especially at night. If you must leave a key with the attendant, never leave any other than the ignition key, and lock valuables in your trunk. If you have a trunk that pops open from inside the vehicle, do not store valuables there.

Walk confidently, with a positive attitude. Hold your purse and/or briefcase securely in the hand which is next to the street. Again, it's a good idea to have your keys ready in case of an attack. It's also a good idea to carry an umbrella or cane to and from your car, even if rain is not predicted. They can be formidable weapons if you are attacked. You may want to carry a whistle or compressed-air horn to blow if attacked. Your best defense, if approached, is to scream.

Once inside the building where you work, go directly to your destination. Don't assume that you are now completely safe from threats.

Ride elevators only when more than one person is aboard with you, and then hope that they are not partners in crime. If you feel uneasy with them, listen to your instincts and exit immediately. When riding the elevator, know where all the operation buttons are and what they do, especially the emergency "STOP" button. If attacked, you can push this button. Most elevators are equipped with intercom systems that are used for communication when the emergency stop button is pushed. So if you push it, yell for help.

Try to remain calm so you will remember to yell which way you are going, up or down, to alert the elevator monitors. When you are already on an elevator, stay alert but look confident and ready. If a strange person(s) enters, such as a drunk off the street, or a person apparently high on drugs, exit immediately. Don't place yourself in jeopardy. In many cities, street people and derelicts enter public buildings to get out of the cold or rain. They usually spend time riding the elevators or visiting the restrooms.

Never walk up or down stairways alone. This is a prime sector for illegal activity. When entering public restroom facilities, be aware of individuals inside. This is another location where criminals can attack. If necessary, leave and come back later, or go to another restroom.

When you leave work for lunch, to shop, or to return home, be sure to practice all security measures. Once home, make sure it's safe to get out of your car. If you're in a parking garage and see strange individuals, drive out and contact police immediately. If you are unable to exit safely, honk your horn, continually. This should get rid of any suspicious characters, and, at the same time, draw attention to you. Remain in your locked car until someone arrives to escort you or until you feel it's safe to exit. Don't forget, it's a good idea to carry your keys firmly in your strong hand to help defend against an assailant.

When taking a taxi home, you can always ask the driver to wait until you have unlocked your door and entered. If you notice an open window or unlocked door, or any suspicious vehicle or person outside your residence, contact the police immediately.

Starting a New Job

When arriving in a new area for the first time, carefully study the environment during nights and weekends to get an idea of activities during those times. In addition, ask to review the company's security policies. If none exist, recommend that some be developed and implemented. Examples of items that should be included:

- Every business should have personnel data on all employees and their families, including emergency information. This should be reviewed and updated periodically.
- Personnel records should be secured.
- Nobody but authorized personnel should have access to them.
- Family members should be able to contact you in the event of an emergency. Provide them with complete written instructions.

Occupations and Their Hazards

Since much of today's crime takes place in the "white collar" business section (banks, drugstores etc.), let's look closely at several occupations that have continually been targeted by criminals. Their examples will help others devise step-by-step strategies to deter and counter threats. Although the conditions cited may in some instances seem extreme, each of them reflects the reality of today's threats.

The Executive

The traditional pressures associated with executive-level jobs have been compounded in recent years by a new concern: the possibility of kidnapping or assassination. Many executives or members of their families have been victimized for economic or political reasons.

When a high-level corporate official is chosen as a kidnap victim, extortion is used for economic gain. The criminal has two main considerations in a case like this: safety, and money. In the few kidnapping cases that occur in the United States, the kidnapper rarely risks his life for the ransom. The terrorist, on the other hand, is out to gain attention for his cause. Most are highly trained and would readily die for their cause, or blow up a bus load of innocent people. Life, for them, has less value than death in the line of "duty."

It is vital that corporations design effective executive protection programs to prevent criminal and terrorist acts. Such programs are usually the responsibility of the firm's security department.

The executive's family is open to exploitation as well, and must be fully aware of the dimensions of these external threats. A complete executive protection plan should include procedures for all company employees and their families, and be practiced regularly, especially abroad.

The following recommendations identify key areas of concern.

Who Qualifies as a Target?

- Are you or your family wealthy?
- Are you an important executive of a large corporation?
- Does your firm have facilities overseas?
- Do you travel extensively?
- Do you travel overseas?
- Do you own stock in your firm?
- Do you serve on the board of directors of an international firm?
- What is the state of the country your firm is located in? Is a political or military overthrow possible? If so, what might happen to you?
- Do you hold office or are you involved in any community organizations or projects?
- Would any person or organization stand to improve their position by kidnapping or murdering you?
- Have you or your corporation taken a political stance that is highly publicized, especially on foreign affairs?
- Has your corporation experienced labor disputes and/or been boycotted or picketed by organizations opposed to its activities?
- Have you received any threats or experienced extortion in the past?

If most of your answers to these questions were yes, you must realistically consider yourself, or a member of your family or firm, a potential target.

Prevention Policies

Here are some ideas to seriously consider:

- Develop codes between family members, servants, and company staff to use in warning each other in case of trouble. These codes must remain secret and be protected regularly (e.g., chauffeur verbally or visually signals executive of trouble).
- If possible, avoid public transportation systems.
- When traveling by air, always use United States carriers if possible.
- Never publicize your flight plans or itinerary.
- Allow only family or trusted associates to know schedules, etc.
- Never change flight schedules at the last minute without notifying appropriate personnel.
- Have someone pick up tickets for you, or arrive early and purchase prior to flight.
- When changing planes, or departing from a location, move confidently and quickly.
- Always avoid set patterns and routines. Change activities as necessary.
- Install alarm systems on all personal vehicles.
- Warn private staff/servants to be alert for unusual or strange activities.
- Chauffeurs should inspect vehicles daily, prior to operation, and double as bodyguards.
- Make sure that all vehicle hood latches are controlled from inside.
- Place a bolt through the tail pipe of all vehicles, to keep explosives from being placed inside.
- Train your chauffeur in defensive driving techniques.

- Keep corporate planes or boats under lock and key; install alarms; check daily.
- Park all vehicles indoors in a controlled, guarded location. Continual camera monitoring should be maintained.
- Never mark executive parking spots with names. Use a varying number system.
- Caution executive and family members not to advertise their location and vehicle by sporting a "personal" license plate that spells out their name or corporation. This goes for status symbols such as club memberships which could be used as identifiers.
- Install alarm systems for corporate buildings.
- Limit the number of accesses to business facilities.
- Remember that key control is critical.
- Control access to buildings and offices by using an effective pass and identification system.
- Escort all visitors.
- Install electronic remote lock switches to control access to sensitive areas from inside the area.
- Install bullet-resistant barriers at the reception area.
- Establish a code system for the receptionist and all other employees for notification in the event of an emergency (e.g., illegal attempt to enter facility).
- Escort hired janitorial/maintenance personnel to all locations.
- Lock all electrical/circuit boxes securely to prevent unauthorized entry.
- Closely monitor mail for letter bombs and potentially dangerous packages.
- Keep news releases about corporation activities and personnel brief, and *never* reveal sensitive plans or activities of the organization or its members and their families. Monitor financial and promotional news for unwanted disclosures.

All foreign travel should be carefully planned, and passports and visas kept in order. It is essential to:

- Understand the customs and laws of the country you are visiting.
- Rent vehicles rather than draw attention to yourself with a corporate limousine.
- Know the language or have an interpreter with you.
- Know whom you are contacting.
- Know the location of the U.S. Embassy.
- Carry the currency of the country. (In many countries it is illegal to spend U.S. dollars.)

The Store Manager/Clerk

Most robberies occur just prior to the opening and closing of a business. It's prime time because few customers are around to witness or interfere with the criminal.

The businesses often marked as pushovers are small stores, including the 24-hour operations. Not only are there few customers around; the manager or clerk is usually alone, or aided by only one other employee.

Some stores will always be more vulnerable to attack than others due to their location and clientele. For most, however, robbery attempts can be limited or deterred by effective security measures.

What Can an Owner/Manager Do?

- Provide proper lighting inside and out, especially behind the store. Darkness attracts and conceals criminals.
- Install adequate locks and alarms, and test their effectiveness regularly.
- Make sure that the parking lot and service areas (e.g., gas pumps) are well-lighted and can be clearly observed.

- Keep store windows free of advertisements to allow clear observation from outside by police or security patrols.

- Remove large quantities of cash and checks periodically and place them in a concealed safe for deposit at the bank at the first opportunity.

- Post signs that warn "No cash on hand after X p.m./a.m." or "After X p.m./a.m. no bills over $20.00 will be accepted."

- Never balance or exchange cash drawers in front of customers.

- Consider using a "dummy safe" which contains a convincing amount of cash and checks, with actual funds secured elsewhere.

- Maintain serial numbers of large bills received.

- Establish a check-cashing policy and make sure that employees strictly adhere to it.

- Vary the route and carrier of bank deposits. Deposit during daylight hours.

- Set up an effective key-control system and check keys regularly.

- Install steel mesh or bars on windows, doors, and lights.

- Install bullet-proof/resistant barriers between office counters and customers.

- Keep high-value items out of windows to guard against criminals breaking the glass to grab the item.

- Install effective viewing mirrors, cameras, and one-way glass.

- Consider the use of a guard dog to patrol the premises after hours. Clearly post "Beware of Dog" warning signs.

- Establish an effective code system that allows employees to warn each other — both visibly and verbally — of trouble.

- Open and close the store with a minimum of two employees. One enters and turns off the alarm system and turns on the lights. Another waits outside for the signal that all is well. If the entering employee fails to show within an established time, the second employee calls the police. Reverse this policy when closing.

- If the store owner/manager receives a call to return to the store once it is closed, he should always notify another senior employee to meet him there and call the police to inform them of suspicious activity. Once inside, and prior to departure, if everything is okay, he should call the police within a set time period to tell them so.

- Verify *all* calls received prior to departing for the store.

- Make sure that all employees understand that they should never argue or struggle with a troublemaker. They, or a customer, could be injured. Call police.

- Employees who are physically threatened or robbed should comply with all demands (use common sense), and cooperate fully if their lives are in danger. Never make any sudden moves. Remain calm and try to observe the criminal closely for a complete description of him and any weapon.

- When accepting a "bad check," an "unauthorized credit card," or counterfeit money from a *known* problem customer, or from one threatening injury:

  1. Try to refuse tactfully, but accept if threatened.

  2. Let them depart from the store.

3. Observe which vehicle they enter, record the vehicle description, license number, and the direction of departure.

4. Record the criminal's description.

5. Call the police immediately.

6. Brief other employees to be on the look-out for the criminal.

The Drugstore Pharmacist

Approximately 90 percent of drugstore robberies committed each year occur in the pharmacy department. Armed theft for the purpose of sale or personal use is a growing problem throughout the United States. Theft is committed at all times of the day and night.

Some stores allow customers to phone the pharmacist in "emergency" situations after closing time. Each time a pharmacist responds to this kind of request, he is placing his life in danger.

What Can Drugstore Owners and Pharmacists Do?

- Recognize the growing problem of drug abuse and the threat that makes them obvious targets for users and pushers.

- Educate and train employees in precautionary and preventive measures to deter crime.

- Do not respond to telephone requests for prescriptions by meeting the customer at the store.

- See that every employee receives training in spotting, observing, and reporting suspicious-looking shoppers.

- Make it clear to every employee that he or she should not attempt to interfere with or thwart a robbery at the risk of personal injury or injury to customers.

- Warn employees to be on the lookout for nervous customers who continually walk around and glance towards the pharmacy area. If these persons repeat their visits, especially during opening and closing hours or at shift changes, the new shift of employees should be alerted to their presence and given a brief description of their activities. Employees should attempt to observe their method of transportation and notify the police.

- When in doubt, lock up.
- Limit the amount of narcotics and other dangerous drugs kept on hand. Order only what you need.
- Do not arrange drugs in logical, identifiable order; this allows unauthorized individuals to locate them easily.
- Limit access to the pharmacy area to employees.
- Do not allow customers to watch the pharmacist fill prescriptions.
- Do not leave filled prescriptions within sight or reach.
- Notify police immediately if a prescription request is fraudulent.
- Maintain adequate staffing.
- Make frequent bank deposits.
- Install adequate viewing mirrors, cameras, and one-way glass.
- Install bullet-proof/resistant barriers.
- Keep store windows clear for internal viewing by police and security patrols, especially the pharmacy area.
- Install electronic remote lock switches to control access to the pharmacy area.
- Advertise that only small amounts of drugs are kept on hand.

Violence in the Work Place

Up to now, this book has been concerned with what could be defined as an external criminal threat - those threats that await us outside of our family, our homes, our schools and jobs. We don't usually expect crime to hit from within, from the friends and associates we work with daily. However, every day more and more we read about the disgruntled, frustrated or desperate employee who walked into his boss's office and shot him or fellow workers. This is an internal threat.

Violence from fellow workers often strikes without warning. We fail to see the signs that point to a growing anger or resentment. Much of the violent crime committed in today's work environment is linked to emotional disorder, which is brought on by the tremendous pressure and stresses on the job. People under enormous stress and pressure can lose touch with reality. They see no end to their troubles and often consider suicide as the only way out. Now if this desperation is directly associated with their boss or another co-worker, the idea of murder-suicide seems pretty good. After all, "it's all his fault."

U.S. Department of Labor statistics disclosed that of the 8,500 reported on-the-job fatalities within the United States in 1992, one-sixth of them, or approximately 1,416, were homicides. Statistics taken from another survey, conducted by the Northwestern National Life Insurance Company, indicated that, as of July 1993, 2.2 million American were physically attacked within their workplace, 6.3 million workers were threatened and 16.1 million were harassed in one way or another.

In 1992 alone, on-the-job violence cost employers 4.2 billion dollars in lost work and legal expenses. Workplace violence starts a chain reaction that is felt by everyone within the company, from the stockboy to the Chief Executive Officer. Employees fearing violence claim illness as an excuse for absence. Employees feeling stress develop real illnesses, such as high blood pressure, ulcers, paranoia and depression. Records show that, due to the internal problems that grow and fester as a result of tension and personality conflicts between workers, the overall productivity of businesses can decrease as much as 20 percent. The effects of workplace violence is felt far beyond the pain and suffering of the unfortunate victims. Businesses have been crippled, slowed and forced to close as a result of internal violence. Nobody wins — everybody loses.

What Can Be Done?

The biggest tragedy of workplace violence is that it doesn't have to be. Employers can take appropriate steps to limit the amount of potential violence that suddenly strikes from within the boardrooms, post offices and fastfood chains across the globe.

First, never assume that it can't happen in your office. Employers must recognize early warning signs that could lead to violence. Be alert to personality changes in your employees. Setting unrealistic goals for workers, as well as enforcing unfair disciplinary actions, will trigger emotional reactions. Job evaluations, layoffs and terminations all create a tremendous amount of stress.

Listen to your employees' comments, especially to the threats. When verbal insults or arguments begin to be more aggressive, the situation may be ripe for violence.

While not wanting to admit it, management is often wrong and the employee is often right. One-sided conversations will set the tone for frustration, mistrust and loss of respect. Unhappy workers will not produce at the level that they are capable of, especially when they feel mistreated and unappreciated. Threats, intimidating behavior, pushing and shoving all add up to the company kettle boiling over. Some of it is justified, especially in the eyes of the employee or co-worker.

Alert company leaders have established crisis management plans, which help identify potential violence, and train key employees to defuse potential violent situations. Unfortunately, most crisis management plans are not implemented during a crisis.

Company fitness and exercise programs help reduce tension while creating a healthier attitude and outlook on life.

Professional counseling services and psychological evaluations should be offered to anyone suffering from stress and pressure created on the job or off. Let your employees know that you care about them.

Create an open-door policy to provide recommendations or to simply blow off steam. When employees are treated fairly and are encouraged to participate in the company decision-making process, they are less likely to feel unappreciated. When conflicts develop, they are more likely to look at the situation as the problem rather than a particular person. Establish a company grievance procedure, and "listen" to what your employees have to say.

Supervisors should be trained to observe positive as well as negative performance results. They need to identify those employees who deserve recognition and those employees who are in need of an attitude adjustment or performance motivation.

Employers must carefully interview and screen job candidates for those who obviously demonstrate an unwillingness to take orders or cooperate with supervisors. Security background checks should be included when hiring employees, especially for those positions with a high level of pressure and stress.

Any history of fighting with, or verbal threats against, previous employers, no matter how justified it may appear, should signal a potential risk.

Never break bad news to employees without preparing for it. Expect the worst, and be ready to seek or recommend professional assistance. Try not to make it personal. Have prepared answers for the expected questions. Show concern. If possible, set up a support team. Recruit a medical professional and someone with a personnel or human resource background who can provide you and the employee with vital employment information and options.

Consider installing or upgrading your company security system to monitor potentially violent hot spots or those areas that have previously been subject to violence. Of equal importance is effective, controlled access to your building which should also include an external surveillance camera that would provide visual observation of key points such as company entrance and exit points, outside break areas and parking lots.

Insure that you advise your legal counsel of any incidents that occur, so that appropriate steps can be taken to protect your company, your employees and your future.

Take a look at the co-worker sitting across from you. Anything upsetting him lately? If so, offer him a cup of coffee and talk about it. It just may save your life.

Recognizing Threats In the School Environment

One morning, Tammy decided that she was "old enough" to walk to the school bus in the morning without Mommy. Mommy, not wanting to treat her daughter like a "baby," agreed.

That same morning, as Tammy proudly joined her friends at the stop, a man drove up in his shiny car and asked her if she would like to go with him and get a jelly donut before school. Before the little girl had a chance to consider the nice man's offer, her bus drove up and she hopped aboard.

Needless to say, the shiny car sped off.

Tammy was lucky. Many others innocently succumb to temptation each year, often to become a sad statistic.

The School Environment

Whether they're in a day care center or on a college campus, students face special threats. Criminals select the easiest, most vulnerable victim to attack. The ability to recognize a threat is based on the amount of education and training a student receives, most of which begins at home. As a child matures, his or her attitudes concerning crime prevention should mature also. For the teenager attending high school or the college-bound young adult, experience is the best teacher, especially when applied with common sense.

Day Care Centers, Preschool, and Kindergarten

It's very important for the parents to fully understand the preschool program they are considering. Most states require preschool and kindergarten facilities and their personnel to meet established legal requirements and standards prior to initiating operation. Study all available material on the school or organization. Ask detailed questions of the staff and of parents and children already attending. Consult your local Board of Education or local government authorities for an in-depth evaluation and/or recommendation. Visit the facility. Does it appear safe? Sanitary?

Questions to Ask

- How long has the center or school been established?
- Is it legally recognized, and is authorization for operation available for review?
- What are the qualifications of the staff? (e.g., education, licenses, etc.)
- Is first aid training a requirement for the staff?
- Is a registered nurse, or a staff member qualified in first aid, available?
- Have there been any accidents, injuries, or deaths within the center? If so, why?
- What form of discipline is administered by the staff?
- If outdoor recreational activities exist, are they safe, and are they supervised 100 percent of the time? Is access available to strangers?

Once you feel satisfied that your children will be cared for by a responsible agency, you should be able to rest a little easier. But it is important to constantly continue your review of the facility, faculty, and other children. Question your children about activities in which they become involved. If it sounds like they are participating in unsafe practices, go and observe a day yourself. If, for any legitimate reason you feel your child's safety and well-being are in jeopardy, pull the child out and report violations to the proper authorities immediately.

What To Tell the Staff

- All important data pertaining to your child in case of emergency. This includes a list of illnesses, allergies, symptoms, blood type, doctor, hospital, etc. If the staff is directed by you to give your child required medication, they must understand your directions clearly and must be able to recognize danger signals.

- Leave your full name, address and phone number where you can be reached if you're not at home, and a back-up number of a friend or relative who can assist during an emergency.

- Never allow anyone except designated parents or relatives to pick your child up from the center. If this rule is broken, even once, pull your children out of the center.

- If friends and neighbors are driving the children on a rotating or carpooling basis, make sure they have permission in writing to pick up the children.

If there is a change, it is always a good idea to call the center in advance (same day) to tell them who is picking up your child. If staff is in any doubt, they should call the parents for release approval, or, as a last resort, keep the child at the center until you can come to get him. This may cause a little trouble and time delay, but not when compared with having a stranger kidnap your child. This requirement should allow you to sleep better! If children are regularly picked up by someone other than their parents, this person should be photographed and the photograph kept on file for immediate identification.

What Parents Should Tell Their Children

Along with the normal counseling that parents provide their children, they should tell them to:

- Inform their parents of any problems, or strange or dangerous activities that they become involved with or exposed to.
- Report all strangers who approach them.
- Never leave the center or school with any stranger.
- Never engage in any activity that frightens them or is wrong.

Grades 1-12

The following additional concerns are important for older students:

- How does the student get to and from school?
- What activities does the student engage in before and after school?
- What freedoms are allowed the student (e.g., driving, dating)? Are they safe? Are they appropriate for his age level?
- Is the parent aware of the student's location and times of return?

Student Safety Tips

- Never leave school without your parent's knowledge.
- Never leave school with a stranger.
- Never hitchhike to or from school.
- Lock all lockers (hall and gym). Never give out your combination to friends, or leave the combination on the last number so that it requires only a spin to open it.
- Never take large sums of money or valuables to school.
- Report all crime to the school's main office.

- If you or other students are experiencing emotional difficulties linked to domestic problems or drug and alcohol abuse, or have any other problem, request the assistance of counselors for support and advice.

College

Whether living at home and commuting to a nearby campus, or living away at school, good security habits will protect both your valuables and your life during this period. Plan to combine the safe home environment procedures discussed earlier with the following additional recommendations.

Room/Dorm Security Questions To Consider

- What is the crime history on campus?
- What areas on campus are considered the most dangerous?
- What is the response time of campus police or security?
- Who is responsible for campus security, and what is their professional background?
- Are external doors and access points locked or electronically monitored?
- Are dorm security or supervisory personnel assigned to monitor building entrances?
- Are room doors made of solid construction; do they close automatically and are they self-locking?
- What is the policy regarding non-resident guests?
- Is there a dorm guest log for security purposes?
- Does your room and facility have adequate door and window locks and lighting?
- Do you share your room or facility with another student?
- Does your roommate practice crime prevention?

- Do you have a complete inventory of all your valuables?
- Who else has keys to your room and facility?
- Will the college re-key your room or facility door if requested? Will they allow you to obtain and pay for this service? (It's worth it, even if you have to pay for it yourself.)
- Does your room have a telephone?
- Do you know the local police/security, fire, and rescue telephone numbers? Are they posted on or near your telephone, along with your complete address?
- Is there an emergency fire exit plan in your facility? Do you know where the emergency fire exits are?

Campus Tips

- Make sure that the college student center/administration office maintains your emergency/next of kin information.
- Never travel alone, especially at night.
- Never take shortcuts across campus that are unfamiliar or possibly unsafe.
- Never hitchhike.
- Never run, jog or exercise outside at night alone.
- Always lock your vehicle or bicycle properly.
- Never allow your room to be left unlocked or leave visitors in your room alone.
- Never allow strangers to enter your room.
- Never give your room key to another person.

Check with your college security department for additional advice on crime prevention and security.

Student Right To Know and Campus Security Act of 1990
(Public Law 101-542)

One of the first steps necessary to resolve a problem is to recognize that a problem exists. Unfortunately, many school officials fail to acknowledge the presence of crime on their campuses and have even gone so far as to cover up criminal wrongdoings, for fear of negative publicity for their institution. Parents and students have a right to know what foreseeable dangers exist that could affect them.

The Right To Know and Campus Security Act studies the problem of crime on campus and has found that violent crime has steadily increased over the last several years. It disclosed that 95 percent of all violent crime on campus is alcohol and drug related, and that 80 percent of all crimes on campus were committed by students upon other students.

With the passage of the Student Right To Know and Campus Security Act of 1990 and the Higher Education Amendments of 1992, all post-secondary institutions participating in federal student aid programs are required to disclose campus security policies and crime statistics. They must prepare, publish and distribute these to all students and employees associated with their institution. The information includes policies concerning campus law enforcement, security programs and practices, statistics on criminal incidents, the reporting of drug and alcohol violations and sexual offenses. Post-secondary institutions include technical and trade schools, private and parochial colleges, community and junior colleges and public colleges and universities.

This law extends beyond the campus boundaries to off-campus student organizations as well. Those departments affected will include the campus police and/or security department, student affairs, housing, admissions, recruitment and the campus facilities department.

In addition, all of these institutions are required to submit copies of their statistics to the U.S. Secretary of the Department of Education, who will process the information and report to Congress by September, 1995. Those campus security policies and procedures that appear to be successful will be shared with all institutions, in an effort to improve the overall security posture within and around all college campuses.

As a result of this act, those institutions that have not placed a priority on security are now required to comply with federal regulations. Of the 8,000 post-secondary schools within the United States, only approximately 350 of them previously reported crime statistics to the appropriate authority.

Threats to Teachers

Teachers are under heavy job pressures. More than 80 percent of new teachers who leave their chosen profession do so within a one- to two-year period, often because they fail to establish and maintain discipline within their classrooms. Many feel forced out of teaching and become disenchanted with their original dreams of educating young people. In some cases, teachers do not receive the support they need from their administration for disciplinary actions. Teachers then are vulnerable to the criticism and scorn of angry parents as well as students.

Verbal confrontation can end with the assault of a teacher in a classroom, hallway, or parking lot. If the teacher is not personally attacked, their residence may be vandalized or their family harassed. A teacher should in all cases attempt to avoid an all-out fight. But when faced with a student attempting assault, the teacher should defend against injury while employing passive restraining techniques.

When a teacher feels that he or she may become the target of an angry student, the following precautions should be taken:

- Report possible threats to school administrators and to the police.
- Remain in the company of other teachers.
- Park vehicles in a visible location for protection against vandalism.
- Advise family to be aware of any strange or unusual activity.
- Increase home protection with lights, locks, etc.
- Avoid secluded areas, such as locker rooms and restrooms.

Based on the experiences of teachers who have been faced with disciplinary problems, the following list of recommendations has been developed to help avoid confrontations in the classroom.

- Establish effective communication with students, and get the support of school administration.

- Involve all students in establishing rules for the classroom, but be sure they understand who is the teacher and who is the student. Help students understand that no organization can survive without order and discipline, and explain how nobody wins when there is anarchy.

- Establish a bond of trust, fairness, and respect with your students.

- Make sure the students understand your directions clearly.

- Avoid sarcasm, shouting matches, and embarrassing or chastising a student in front of classmates. You may create a confrontation by backing him into a corner.

- Never threaten punishment unless you are willing to carry it out.

- Identify problem students and determine how to handle them. Recommend counseling when it is obvious that a student is suffering from domestic or drug and alcohol problems. Try to become not just a teacher, but also a friend who is concerned. Students respect this. Identify the dangerous students and take whatever steps are necessary to insure a safe environment for other students and teachers.

- Recognize accomplishments of students and provide positive reinforcement when possible.

- Never underestimate the power a teacher has. Most students look up to teachers and heed their comments. A single recommendation can build — or destroy — a career.

Recognizing Threats In the Recreational Environment

J ack had carried luggage at the sumptuous Oceanview Inn for only three months. His minimum wages, small tips and long, hard hours increased his resentment of the guests who could afford the luxuries he only dreamed of.

With easy access to the room keys, Jack decided one day to get lucky and then get out of town. Stashing jewelry, cash, cameras, and clothing into a suitcase, he was long gone before anything was missed. Not an hour away, Jack was already plotting his next rip-off. "It was so easy to lift the goodies all those trusting tourists left behind," he mused. "It'll be even easier next time!"

Depending on how much time and money people have available, their vacation may range from a one-day shopping spree to a months-long cross-country excursion. But just because we relax and try to forget the daily hustle and bustle we left behind, it doesn't mean that the criminal element is also relaxing. Indeed, professional and amateur criminals alike eagerly await the vacationing tourist, who is temporarily hypnotized by the sights and sounds of the vacation area. Never — especially at vacation time — relax your awareness your immediate environment. (If you're not yet thinking "awareness," you should be by the time you finish this book.)

Effective Planning

Planning for your vacation should include a careful, well-organized checklist of priorities. Too often, an excited family forgets a small essential task or leaves behind a simple object, only to suffer later for the oversight. By taking the time to arrange priorities in a logical, common-sense format, a schedule can be designed to cover the necessary items and lay the groundwork for a safe and enjoyable vacation.

Begin by gathering the family together for a discussion so that everyone can contribute to the vacation checklist. Be sure to cover the entire vacation from beginning to end. By involving each family member you indirectly place responsibility on everyone's shoulders. This makes everyone feel needed, and helps to develop a responsible attitude as well.

Gather the family and cover the basic principles of safety and security. Inform everyone of the potential hazards and dangers that exist, and what to do if exposed to them. Encourage questions and quiz your children about situations that they may run into. To simply say "Stick close," or "Don't talk to strangers," is not enough, even though this is just about all that many families cover during a family outing.

By discussing what could happen, you are likely to prompt questions that will educate your family and prevent involvement in a dangerous situation. Present the question, "What could happen if . . .?" You may be surprised by the answers you receive.

Precautions To Take When Leaving for Vacation

Many homes are broken into and vandalized because the owners made it clear that nobody would be home to stop the thieves. A home that looks occupied stands a better chance of escaping burglary than one that appears deserted.

When you are planning a long vacation, or just an evening out, you must always secure your home. Before you depart, always:

- Inform the police of your impending absence, and ask them, when possible, to patrol the area and keep an eye out for any suspicious activity.

- Leave a key to your home with trusted neighbors, and ask them to inform the police of any suspicious activity.

- Leave several lights on throughout your home. If you are to be gone for a long period of time, use a timer switch to activate the lights, radio and television at different intervals. Make sure that all timer devices are safe, or, as an alternative, ask your neighbor to turn on these appliances for you.

- Leave blinds or shades in their normal positions.

- Arrange to have your lawn mowed, and snow plowed or shoveled from your driveway. Stop newspaper and mail deliveries, or arrange to have them picked up regularly.

- Take all your valuables to a safe deposit box, or leave them with a trusted relative or friend.

- Do not discuss your vacation plans or schedules with anyone except your trusted neighbor or close relative.

- Never leave notes on your door telling when you will return.

- Arrange to have garbage cans used by a neighbor, who will set them out for pick-up.

- If you own two vehicles and take only one on vacation, park the remaining one in the space where the primary vehicle is normally parked.

- Turn the ringer volume down on your telephone.

- Ask your neighbor to make several security checks of your residence while you are gone.

Family Identification

Each member of your family, including the baby, should carry some form of identification. Every person, no matter how old, should carry an identification card (Figure 8-1). The card should include normal identification information, as well as special data such as blood type, allergies, required medication, and information about conditions such as heart trouble or high blood pressure. An identification card can be made for each child at home and encased in plastic. This card can be carried in a variety of ways, including being attached to a necklace or pinned to a piece of clothing.

Figure 8-1

FAMILY IDENTIFICATION

Front

Name _____ Age: _____

Home Address: _____   PHOTO

Home Phone Number: _____

Parents' Names Are: _____

Next of Kin: _____ Phone: _____

Special Medications: _____

_____ Blood Type: _____

Allergies/Reactions: _____

Misc. Data: _____

Back

Daily Itinerary

Temp. Address: (i.e., Hotel/Motel-Room No.) _____

_____

Phone Number: (___)_____

Vehicle ID: Make: _____ Model: _____

Year: _____ Color: _____ License Number: _____

Currently Parked At: _____

Estimated Time of Departure: _____

Family is Currently At: _____

Another good idea is for each vacationing family member to carry a daily itinerary. It would contain temporary data, such as where the family is staying, and vehicle identification, including its current location and what time all are expected to return to the vehicle. This itinerary may be stuffed in a pocket or taped to the back of the member's identification card. Now if "little Johnny" is accidentally separated from Mom and Dad at the amusement park, the good Samaritan or security officer who finds him will have comprehensive information to work with.

Along with providing their identification cards, you must tell your children that if they are separated from you, there are certain people who will help them find you. Tell them to look for a policeman or a person dressed up like one (security guard), while pointing one out to them. If one is not available, then they should approach a concession stand and ask for help. Under no circumstances are they to exit the park *without* Mommy or Daddy!

Special Items

Always double-check before departing from home, to be sure that you have those special items that cannot be easily replaced, such as medicines, an extra pair of glasses or contact lenses, credit cards, etc.

Inventory of Valuables

Before you leave home, also prepare a complete inventory of valuables you are taking with you (camera, radio, etc.) in case they are stolen while on vacation. Be sure to include any identification numbers or codes. Leave one copy with a neighbor or friend, and take another with you.

Public Transportation

If you and your family are planning to travel by public transportation, take the following precautionary measures to help avoid problems:

- Understand all travel plans and transportation transfers completely.

- Lock all luggage and mark it with complete identification, including home address and phone number. Tags can be torn off, so it's best to mark directly on the surface of the luggage.

- Never leave baggage tags on from previous trips. These might lead to a misrouting of your luggage.

- Never travel with contraband or dangerous items.

- Carry travelers checks instead of large sums of cash.

- Obtain insurance on high-value items prior to travel.

- Never leave carry-on luggage (e.g., briefcase, purse) unattended.

- Never leave children unattended.

- Transferring from one bus, train, or plane to another can be a frustrating experience. Plan ahead, and don't be afraid or embarrassed to ask for help.

- Prior to departing on any public transportation, make sure that everyone traveling understands what to do in the event that one family member is separated from the rest of the group, because *it does happen*. Decide on an alternative meeting site at a designated time. For example, let's say that you did get separated from your spouse on the subway; you will now know to immediately travel to the predetermined meeting site, such as the water fountain in the middle of the park on Main Street, one hour from the time of separation.

If you are traveling by train, always secure your belongings prior to leaving your individual compartment. When traveling, especially in crowded situations, keep an eye out for pickpockets, particularly the stranger next to you.

Accommodations

When taking a vacation means staying in a hotel or motel, there are several important items to consider.

Tips for a Safer Stay

- Always try to locate a well-kept hotel or motel in a highly visible, well-lighted area. Avoid back-street locations that can conceal criminals.

- When you check into your lodgings, study all procedures and attitudes towards guests. Poor service in the lobby is a possible indicator of poor room conditions.

- If you are staying in a motel, park directly in front of your assigned room if possible. If poor parking accommodations require you to isolate your vehicle at any great distance, look for another establishment. As a last resort, park in front of the motel office.

- When you have been assigned a room, test the door lock and survey the room closely for security or safety hazards.

- Once inside, close the blinds before unpacking your luggage. There is no need to advertise what you have with you.

- When unloading your vehicle, never leave your room or vehicle unattended if unlocked. If you are alone, take the time to lock the car trunk or door before leaving for your room. Trunks left open while you step inside your room may offer passersby a view of your luggage, as well as a possible free gift.

- Lock anything left in your vehicle inside the trunk. Any highly valuable items should always be locked in the hotel/motel safe, and be sure to get a receipt. NOTE: There are probably many keys that will open your room door. Your room can be opened with the hotel master key by maids, maintenance men, etc. Most hotels warn that you leave items in your room at your own risk, so don't ask for trouble by leaving your camera or watch inside the room when you go out. Many hotel and motel keys are lost or stolen, and the locks are never changed. This creates not only a property risk problem, but a personal risk as well.

- Always use the door lock and security chain when inside your room.

- Be sure to lock your door and double-check it anytime you return to your room, It's also a good idea to place a room chair behind your door to hinder any unexpected entrances. This will not, of course, prevent a person from making a forceful entrance, but it will usually provide enough racket to warn you.

- Never leave children alone in your room or in the lobby.

- If a maintenance man is required, always contact the hotel desk and confirm the worker's identity upon arrival at the door of your room.

- Never flash money around in public.

- Never inform strangers of your employment position or how long you intend to be away.

- Never go to the pool and leave your room key unguarded with your towel.

- Never leave children alone at the pool.

- Never leave children alone in the restroom or the shower room. Accompany them or wait outside for them.

- When leaving your room, expect maid service, so be sure to secure your property accordingly.

- Never walk to your room in the dark. Stay in the light, and ask for an escort if you are concerned.

- Leave a light on if you intend to return at night. Upon returning to your room, peek inside the window, if possible, to insure your room is empty. If the light is off, don't panic. Possibly the maid was in earlier and turned it off; however, don't take any chances. It could mean someone is waiting inside for you. Always enter with caution. By all means never enter a room when you think someone could be waiting inside.

- When parked at an out-of-state hotel/motel, consider your vehicle license plates. The criminal knows that you are an easy target, just passing through.

If your room or vehicle is broken into, notify the local police immediately. Provide the police with a complete description of items stolen (from the inventory list you prepared prior to departure). You probably will never see your property again, but if, by chance, it is recovered, the police should notify you. Always get a complete copy of the police report/investigation to keep for future use, as well as for insurance purposes.

When You Check Out

- Make sure to check your room thoroughly for items you may have forgotten.
- Obtain valuables secured in the hotel safe.
- Pay your bill, return your key, and leave the souvenir towel or ash tray in the room where it belongs.

Activities

When involved in activities like sightseeing or visiting the zoo or amusement park, be sure everyone has an identification card. Make sure everyone understands the planned activities and knows what to do if separated. A time schedule should be set up and adhered to. Each person should be able to remember what the others are wearing (identify colors, etc.), so that they can locate one another if separated. Always inform each other of unscheduled activities, and never split up without both taking someone along and informing the other family members where you plan to be. Inform each other when entering a restroom, and leave your purse or souvenirs with another family member.

Make sure to carry only the money you need, and never place it in just one pocket. Place your credit cards and cash in separate front pockets, remaining alert for pickpockets and purse snatchers. All purses, cameras, etc., should be securely held and never left unattended. It is also a good idea to locate a police or security officer and identify him to your children so they are able to recognize him, if needed.

Coming Home

- If you find a door or window open, do not enter. Use your neighbor's phone and call the police immediately. The criminal may still be inside.

- Conduct a complete inspection of your home and all property.

- If you arrive home by taxi, ask the driver to accompany you to your door.

- Always have your keys in hand for extra protection as you open the door.

- Keep a sharp watch out for strangers or strange vehicles nearby. If you notice any unusual disturbance or have any uneasy feelings, call the police.

- Let your neighbor know you're home (especially if returning in the middle of the night) or slide a note under his door.

- Now unpack your luggage, put on your robe and slippers, click your heels together three times, and repeat, "There's no place like home . . ."

Consumer Fraud: Beware of the Wolf In Sheep's Clothing

A 70-year-old grandmother was called on by a salesman trying to sell her an insurance policy that offered unlimited reimbursement for medical bills, at a cost of only $10.00 per month. The only thing Grandma had to do was give the salesman $2,500 up front in order for the policy to take effect.

Wise Grandma excused herself to "turn off the stove." Instead, she made a quick phone call to the insurance company, only to discover that her "salesman" was wanted for stealing blank policy certificates. She then made another call to the police. While she poured the salesman his second cup of tea, police arrived and took him away.

Beware the Wolf in Sheep's Clothing

Each year thousands of unsuspecting families become victims of fraud. Con artists thrive on schemes, scams, rip-offs, and swindles, walking away from trusting individuals with millions of their hard-earned dollars. Most of the victims who feel the sting of these scams find it too embarrassing to admit that they were fooled, and often fail to report the crime to their local police.

What we are talking about here is the deliberate act of intent to mislead a potential customer into purchasing a product that is usually of poor quality, or forcing the signing of a contract under high-pressure sales tactics.

This is not to say that legitimate sales people do not exist; of course they do. What you need to watch out for are the unethical, crooked flim-flam artists who claim to represent legitimate businesses.

Who is the Victim?

Anyone can unknowingly fall prey to a con artist, but, in some cases, specific targets are preyed on because of their inexperience and obvious weaknesses.

The senior citizen is a prime example. Most seniors are very friendly and trusting, and enjoy the company of anyone who shows an interest in conversation with them. Since the fear of crime on the street forces many to remain in the confines of their homes or retirement center, they find it convenient to buy products from door-to-door sales people or through the mail.

Unfortunately, errors in judgment can result from handicaps such as sight or hearing loss. Thus, the elderly are frequently the targets of high-pressure tactics to sign on the dotted line.

Another group heavily favored to be victimized are young people. Their lack of experience with high pressure sales tactics can make them easy marks for the experienced con.

Then there are the rest of us — the housewife who gets taken advantage of by a service station mechanic, or the businessman who gets ripped off by a plumber, electrician, or office-supply dealer.

Methods of Fraud

Door-to Door Salespersons

- Beware of the so-called "free gift." It's usually a gimmick to get you to buy something expensive.

- Any time you purchase an item from a door-to-door salesperson that costs $25 or more, you are supposed to receive a written contract, along with at least two Notice of Cancellation forms. If you should change your mind, you have up to three days to cancel your order. (Check with your state laws.)

- Anyone selling a product door-to-door should be checked out through the Better Business Bureau or Consumer Affairs Office.

- Never purchase medical supplies, insurance, or equipment without first checking out the company. Never purchase "medicines" from salespersons.

- Never buy land without seeing it first.

- Never sign a work contract for home repairs without checking the business out through the Better Business Bureau or Consumer Affairs Office.

- Beware the person who says one thing outside your home, but once inside, quickly or schemingly changes his motives for being there. Someone who will lie or trick you to gain entrance will also stoop to trickery to gain a sale. This person may also be posing as a representative for a survey or opinion poll, while actually casing or studying your home for his next robbery.

- Never buy a product because the salesperson uses scare tactics like "It's for your own good." Never be pressured into any sale.

- Never sign a contract without reading it and understanding it fully. It is always wise to seek legal advice on any contract.

- If the salesperson avoids your questions or does not have the answers, do not purchase the product.

Mail Order Scams

- Always understand what you are buying and how much it is going to cost you.

- Never send cash through the mail.

- Federal law requires most mail order firms to fill your order within thirty days unless stated otherwise. If you fail to receive your order within the thirty days, you may cancel, and the company must refund your money within seven days.

- Be concerned about the "free gift" offers or the grand prize you have just won, especially if you did not enter the contest. Most of these techniques are used to lure you into buying products you never wanted.

- If you receive something by mail that you did not order, don't open it. Mark it "Return to Sender" and mail it back.

- "Earn a degree at home." Many advertised home study or improvement courses promise an "accredited degree" (but accredited by whom?), with the possibility of helping you locate a job after successfully completing the course. These programs usually request a fairly large enrollment fee (non-refundable) and offer no guarantees. Legitimate home study and college-level degree programs do operate by mail, but read the fine print to be sure.

Home Improvement/Repair

Watch out for the person who attempts to convince you that you need home repairs that they can perform at a special rate. Common examples: resurfacing your driveway with a cheap resurfacing material, fixing your roof, or building an addition onto your home. These people usually require an advance, if not payment in full, prior to work, then skip out of town leaving the work half completed, if started at all. If the work is completed, it is usually with inferior materials, which last just long enough for the contractor to get away. Any guarantees offered should be closely examined, and the firm's credentials confirmed before you sign any contract. Again, contact the local Better Business Bureau or Consumer Affairs Office.

Health Insurance

The cost of medical services has risen dramatically. For many, especially senior citizens receiving Medicare, the necessary treatment is unaffordable. But all one has to do is read magazine articles and watch television to realize that there are many different insurance programs available that will cover expenses that their current medical insurance and/or Medicare will not.

Legitimate? Maybe, but too many are designed for only one reason: to take advantage of those in need. There are good insurance programs advertised, but are they exactly what you need? Take the proper time to investigate them. Write your state Insurance Commissioner or Better Business Bureau. Above, all, before you purchase an insurance policy, be sure it contains what it is supposed to cover, and make sure you understand it completely.

Con Games

Bait-and-Switch Routine: Some businesses offer or advertise a particular product for a certain price. When you try to purchase this product you are told, "We're all sold out," or, "It's really not what you need." Then the salesperson attempts to sell you another, similar product for more money, usually playing on your pride and conscience to "spend a little more for the added protection or performance. Your family is worth it."

Earn Money at Home: Many ads offer "large sums of money in a few short weeks for working in the privacy of your own home!" Most only want your money, in advance, and then supply you with worthless advice, or impractical and expensive "get rich quick" schemes.

The Pigeon Drop: This is a very old and effective con game that has stolen more money from the unwary than most others combined. First, a stranger begins a conversation with you. He or she will always be neatly dressed, and will be very polite and courteous. Pretty soon they tell you that they have stumbled onto a very large sum of money, and eventually will offer you a share. "There is enough for the both of us," they will say. Once you agree to help, or indicate you would like to make some easy money, you will be asked to put up some "good faith" money before you can receive your part of the cash. Once you provide your good faith money, you'll never see it or the swindler again.

The Obituary Column Trick: A con man will read of the recent death of a spouse or relative in the paper. He will then arrive in person or send a request in the mail referring to a debt that was left unpaid by the recently departed, and request payment. Usually, the victim is still in mourning and pays the bill before it is completely checked out. Any legitimate person or organization should understand the delay in payment in a case such as this. Also, beware the person who arrives with a very expensive bible or other related object, possibly with an engraving or inscription on it from the deceased, with instructions that it is to be delivered to the surviving spouse upon death, *cash on delivery*. Surely, if your loved one had taken the necessary time to order a gift for an occasion such as this, it would have been paid for in advance. Request an order invoice, or receipt, with a valid signature on it to confirm the sale, or forget it.

Consumer Rights

The following is a look at common everyday concerns that affect everyone across the country. The following consumer rights apply to most U.S. states, but you should research exactly what rights exist in your area. This can be done by contacting your local Consumer Affairs Office.

Auto Repair

All dealers or service stations providing repairs must:

- Give you a written estimate if the cost is over $25 unless you turn it down in writing. The final charges may not be more than 10 percent over the original estimate unless you authorized such repair and additional costs. (Providers of certain professional services, such as lawyers, doctors, and dentists, are not required to provide estimates.)
- Provide you with a copy of any document you have signed.
- Provide you a complete list of all itemized items and their costs, including labor. They cannot charge you for things not listed or related to

repairs unless you were notified in advance, and they cannot claim a repair that is not or was not needed.

- Provide you with all replaced parts unless you were told in advance that they would not be returned, or indicated you did not want them.

Telephone Requests for Repairs or Service

When you request information pertaining to repairs or service over the phone, you are authorized to receive estimates orally, and then to receive a written one before any work is performed. In addition, when calling for towing service, you must be informed of the service charge, cost per mile, and any other related charge for service.

Refunds

Every person is entitled to a full refund for any item purchased by cash or check when it is returned in its original condition, unless a sign was posted conspicuously that stated you must have a receipt, or that there is a "No Refund" policy.

Deposits

Any time you place a deposit on an item, you are entitled to a dated receipt and information that specifically states the time limit it will be held for you, the total cost, and whether the deposit is refundable or not.

Turn the Wolves Away

Beware of:

- High pressure sales tactics, such as "Buy now, or forget it," or "Buy now because tomorrow the price will go up."
- "Act now, and get your free gift."
- "Earn high wages quickly and easily in the comfort and privacy of your own home."
- "You have been selected as one of our winners . . ."
- "Cash only," and usually in advance.
- Sales that offer no guarantees.

Never:

- Sign a contract until you have reviewed it thoroughly or have had it reviewed for you.
- Agree to withdraw money from your bank account based on a request from a so-called bank representative to help "catch a dishonest employee."
- Engage in any scheme that offers "quick and easy cash." Verify through at least two reputable sources.
- Allow anyone into your home without proper identification, especially those individuals who appear strange or under the influence of alcohol or drugs. When in doubt, leave them out.
- Open any mail not addressed to you or that you did not order. Mark "Return to Sender" and let the postal service return it with no charge to you.

Always:

- Get a signed, dated receipt for any item you purchase.
- Keep all paperwork related to a purchase.
- When in doubt, contact the sales company supplying the product to confirm a sales representative or to have your questions answered and any complaints taken care of.
- When considering purchasing a product, stop and think if you really need it, and if it is reliable.
- Be sure all family members and house employees are aware of fraud and how to handle it.
- Get a written estimate when requesting any repairs and services.
- Learn to say NO!
- Report any suspicious activity or individual(s) to the police immediately.
- Contact your local Better Business Bureau or Consumer Affairs Office when in doubt about any

sales activity as well as to confirm the reliability and performance of a product.

- Determine if a sales company is local. Obtain a complete address and phone number, and confirm it if you feel concerned.

- Report a fraud to your local police, the Better Business Bureau, and Consumer Affairs Office.

- Consider taking fraudulent persons and businesses to Small Claims Court.

Remember, very rarely will you get something for nothing. Somewhere you will pay the price. Learn to fight back by being on the lookout for fraud. Slam the door in its face and send the con artist away with the knowledge that the consumer is becoming harder to swindle.

For More Information, Contact:

- Federal Trade Commission: for information pertaining to false or deceptive sales activities, when the manufacturer of the product is located out of state.

- U.S. Postal Service: for information and advice pertaining to mail fraud or violations.

- Better Business Bureau.

- Consumer Affairs Office.

- State Attorney General's Office.

- U.S. Consumer Product Safety Commission.

- State Public Utility Commission: for utility problems.

- Local police.

- County Prosecutor's Office.

10

Protecting Your Transportation

Pulling into a convenience store for a quick cup of coffee, Jeff hopped out of his Dad's new convertible, leaving the keys in the ignition. "I'll only be a second," he thought to himself.

Snapping the lid on his coffee cup, he paid the clerk and headed outside only to watch his Dad's new toy disappear into the evening darkness.

Motor Vehicle Theft

One of the most frequent crimes being committed in every neighborhood around the country is motor vehicle theft. One vehicle is stolen every 20 seconds. Whether taken for parts, a joy ride or for transportation out of the state, motor vehicle theft accounted for 13 percent of all property crimes in the United States in 1992. During this year, a total of 193,775,000 vehicles were registered throughout the country; 1,610,800 were stolen. Profitable to the tune of 7.6 billion dollars, experts report that one out of every 120 vehicles falls victim to theft.

Out of the 171,269 arrests that were made for motor vehicle theft in 1992, 44.3 percent were of young adults between the ages of 15 and 19.

There's a lot you can do to keep the amateur from stealing your vehicle, but if the professional wants it, he will usually get it. The best you can do is to practice good security habits, and maintain appropriate insurance coverage in case of loss. Above all, keep complete, accurate, and up-to-date records on all vehicles. At a minimum, maintain the following:

- Vehicle identification number.
- Hull identification number (for boats).
- Year, make, and model.
- Engine size.
- Color.
- License number and state (for both vehicle and trailer, if applicable).
- Any unusual details or markings.

If your vehicle is stolen, report it to the police immediately with this identification information.

When Purchasing a Vehicle

When you decide to buy a new or used vehicle, always be sure you are not getting one that is "hot," or stolen. Always buy from a reputable dealer. Private sales are fine, but beware of the smooth, "too good to be true" deals. If you are suspicious, contact the police.

If you buy your car from a private individual, make sure that the person you deal with has a listed address and phone number. Check all paperwork and be sure listed serial/vehicle identification numbers match, and that they have not been tampered with or changed. Also be sure the license plates are valid. If in doubt, check with the local police. Do all the keys fit, and do they work properly? Always request a receipt at the time of purchase, along with a witnessed bill of sale that includes all the necessary data (social security number, identification number, odometer reading).

Following is a list of tips to help deter the theft of your vehicle. The easiest and usually most effective technique is to simply lock all doors, roll up the windows, and remove the ignition key! In addition, always:

- Park in a visible location, away from alleys, abandoned buildings, etc.
- If you have a garage, use it and keep it locked.
- Park in a well-lighted area.
- Use a vehicle alarm system if possible.
- Advertise with a sticker that your vehicle has an alarm system.
- Lock all valuables (CB, tape deck, shopping bags) in the trunk.
- Use an anti-theft lock or device to lock the steering column when possible.
- When parked at a curb, always angle the front tires into the curb at approximately a 45-degree angle, preventing easy towing by thieves.
- Do not leave a vehicle abandoned or parked in any location (away from home) for long periods of time.
- Apply ignition "cut-off" devices, or pull the coil wire from the distributor when leaving a vehicle at an unknown location for several hours.
- Never leave the vehicle title or registration inside your vehicle.
- Place special markings on your vehicle to assist in identification if stolen and then recovered. Drop a business or identification card down inside the door for future identification.
- When parking in a commercial lot, never give the attendant all your keys, just the ignition/door key; always remove any valuables. Most lots warn that they are not responsible for lost or missing items. Try to avoid this type of parking lot if possible.
- Check license plates, especially if from out of town, to insure that they have not been stolen or switched.

One of the most accurate books on vehicle theft statistics is "*The Fact Book 1994: Property/Casualty Insurance Facts,*" published by The Insurance Information Institute, 1994.

The following data was selected from this fact book highlighting the area of insured automobile theft losses in the U.S. in 1992:

"The 1992 cars and their parts are stolen less frequently but cost more per claim than new models in any pervious year. An average of $3,320 is paid out for each theft claim for a 1992 car, according to the Highway Loss Data Institute (HLDI), which studied insurance theft records.

"HDLI suggests these thefts reflect two different patterns: thefts of components and thefts of the complete vehicle. Mercedes and Chevrolet Corvette convertibles, for example, have very high average loss payments per claim, indicating that many of their thefts involve the entire vehicle. Nearly half of the claims for the Mercedes SL series exceed $50,000 giving it the worst overall theft losses.

"In contrast, most Volkswagen and Cadillac models have very high claim frequencies but low average loss payments per claim, indicating many losses from theft of components. Together, these two quite different makes account for the top 10 models with the most frequent thefts.

"Thefts of radios contribute heavily to the poor results of the Volkswagen models. At more than eight times the average, the Volkswagen Golf/GTI has the highest frequency of theft claims. High claim frequencies for Volkswagen models have been a consistent finding over the past 10 years of HLDI theft analyses.

"The Mercury Sable's station wagon and four-door models have the lowest claim frequencies, only about one-fourth that of all cars combined. Most of the other cars with low theft claim frequencies are also midsize station wagons and four-door sedans.

"Among vans, pickups and utility vehicles, large utility vehicles have by far the worst insurance theft losses: Their average loss payment per insured vehicle year is more than seven times the average for cars. The Toyota Land Cruiser, an intermediate utility vehicle, has the highest theft losses of any individual van, pickup or utility vehicle — nearly 12 times the average for all passenger cars and an average loss payment per claim of over $20,000."

MOTOR VEHICLE THEFTS AND DOLLAR LOSSES BY STATE, 1992							
State	Thefts	$ change from 1991	Dollar loss	State	Thefts	% change from 1991	Dollar loss
Ala.	14,983	.8	$80,159,050	Mont.	1,923	15.4	5,644,005
Alaska	2,918	-4.1	16,868,958	Neb.	3,225	-4.8	13,099,950
Ariz.	31,481	-2.5	134,518,313	Nev.	9,225	10.5	41,101,455
Ark.	7,900	-2.4	42,565,200	N.H.	2,165	-11.1	10,335,710
Calif.	320,112	1.4	1,255,159,152	N.J.	63,524	-11.6	364,627,760
Colo.	17,662	22.6	77,536,180	N.M.	5,974	11.4	31,070,774
Conn.	23,700	-9.5	136,085,400	N.Y.	168,922	-6.8	712,344,074
Del.	2,109	-17.3	9,439,884	N.C.	19,613	-2.7	87,336,689
D.C.	9,118	12.1	34,885,468	N.D.	950	18.0	3,339,250
Fia.	111,685	7.4	589,808,485	Ohio	51,886	-5.2	102,786,166
Ga.	38,913	-3.9	160,282,647	Okla.	16,601	-6.1	61,307,493
Hawaii	4,351	14.1	7,718,674	Ore.	15,881	14.6	70,003,448
Idaho	1,679	-9.4	6,826,814	Pa.	56,171	-2.5	280,237,119
Ill.	71,976	-4.8	431,856,000	R.I.	7,463	-6.4	36,203,013
Ind.	25,496	-2.2	184,438,064	S.C.	12,443	-9.7	NA
Iowa	4,474	-6.2	16,696,968	S.D.	719	-11.0	2,933,520
Kan.	8,169	6.7	25,119,675	Tenn.	28,935	-4.8	134,663,490
Ky.	8,128	2.0	38,990,016	Texas	145,071	-11.5	783,818,613
La.	26,926	10.4	213,577,032	Utah	4,313	1.1	16,605,050
Maine	1,778	-11.8	7,039,102	Vt.	600	-26.7	1,732,200
Md.	35,654	0.4	185,686,032	Va.	19,488	-8.4	106,014,720
Mass.	47,416	-13.9	234,898,864	Wash.	24,214	8.6	83,536,156
Mich.	59,057	-7.2	467,790,497	W.Va.	2,968	-5.8	15,395,016
Minn.	15,911	-1.2	74,065,705	Wis.	21,605	-0.1	78,058,865
Miss.	8,797	18.6	33,076,720	Wyo.	701	-1.4	2,827,133
Mo.	25,831	-10.3	112,674,822				

NA: Supplemental Data (monetary values) were not available for South Carolina; therefore, dollar values could not be provided.
Source: Federal Bureau of Investigaton.

Motorcycles and Bicycles

A large number of bikes are stolen each year for the same reasons that cars and trucks are. Too many are left unattended and unlocked, which make them easy targets for the thief. If you want your property secure, you have to take proper measures to keep it secure.

To start with, record the serial number/identification number of your bike and keep it stored with other valuable papers, so that you can, when appropriate, provide the police with a complete description. Many police departments have bicycle registration programs set up for this purpose. Take a color photo and keep it with the other identification data.

In addition to the existing serial number, or if no identification number exists, you might want to engrave your social security number or other important number on your bike to help identify it.

Always carry a lock and chain that will secure your bike effectively. Make sure the lock is practical and efficient, and the chain is strong enough to withstand a good deal of punishment. When using a chain or cable, always secure the front and back wheels to a solid, permanent fixture. On most motorcycles, there is a front fork lock built in, or a place for a padlock, that should be utilized every time you leave your bike. Never leave your bike lying around. You can also park your bike between a wall and your car. This will slow down a thief.

Boat Theft

Boat theft is on the increase, and is fast becoming a very lucrative illegal business. Thousands of private and commercial vessels are stolen each year. When entire boats cannot be successfully taken, their engines, instruments, and other expensive parts are removed. It is estimated that over $60 million is lost annually in the theft of boats and related marine equipment

Measures can and must be taken to help deter, and in some cases eliminate, the chance of theft. All boats are required by state and federal law to have individual titles and registrations. These requirements simplify the tracing of stolen vessels and increase the likelihood of return to the rightful owner.

Titling and registration is currently required in 45 of the 50 United States. Unfortunately, uniform guidelines have not yet been established between states to provide effective boat titling procedures and records systems that would help states determine valid ownership of stolen boats.

The 1971 Federal Boat Safety Act mandated that all boats manufactured for sale within the United States be marked by the manufacturer with a twelve-character "Hull Identification Number" (HIN). This number is used to help the manufacturer maintain quality control of inventory, and also to protect the buyer in ways that allow proper identification of model year.

Identification and serial numbers are extremely important in verifying ownership, but might not always be necessary if owners would take proper measures to secure their property. Consider how simple it can be for a thief to back his vehicle up to a boat mounted on a trailer, hook it up, and drive away. This happens in broad daylight, not just in the dead of night. The same is true for boats left unlocked and unattended, floating in the water. Then it is even simpler for a thief, since all he has to do is start it up and speed away to a waiting trailer.

Anti-Theft Tips for Boats

- Understand your state and local laws pertaining to boat ownership/operation.
- Understand existing systems to help prevent theft of boats and equipment.
- Know how to report stolen equipment, and to whom.
- Keep up-to-date photos of your boat and equipment.
- Maintain a complete inventory of equipment and a detailed listing of serial numbers, hull identification numbers, etc. Affix your own private identification marks in secret locations.
- Maintain adequate insurance coverage.
- Lock at least two parts of the trailer to a permanent fixture.

- Chain the engine securely, or remove it and lock it inside a building or the cabin of the boat.
- If your boat is mounted on a trailer parked in your yard or driveway, make sure that it cannot be towed away by unauthorized means.
- Never leave your boat ignition key with the boat.
- Remove a wheel from the trailer if it is to be parked for a long period of time.
- Remove the battery.
- Never leave a "For Sale" sign in a parked boat. Passersby might assume the thief is a prospective purchaser.
- Report any suspicious activity or individuals around your boat or the marina to the police immediately.

When your boat is stolen, notify:

- Local and state police, who will in turn contact the National Crime Information Center (NCIC) and the FBI.
- U.S. Coast Guard, who will also notify NCIC and the FBI.
- Marina or storage manager and dealer from whom boat was purchased, who will in turn notify the Marine Trade Association (hot lists) and boat manufacturer.
- Insurance company, who will notify the National Theft Reporting and Recovery Bureaus.
- Neighbors and nearby marina.

Aircraft Theft

Stealing aircraft usually requires a bit more sophistication than stealing land or water vehicles, but it is steadily increasing in popularity among criminals. The big advantage in aircraft theft is that the thief is not restricted by roads or water. All that is necessary to "fly" away with a plane is knowledge of piloting (there are thousands of registered and unregistered pilots throughout the United States). If the thief himself can't fly, he can easily find a partner in crime with the necessary skills to do so, or simply abduct the owner/pilot and force him to pilot the plane to an unknown destination.

Once in the air, the criminal may be requested by control towers to provide certain flight data, in addition to making periodic radio contacts. This is accomplished by providing false information, or by forcing the hijacked owner to respond with the necessary communications. Aircraft are stolen for many reasons, and an alarming number are used for illegal drug trafficking. Most are flown out of state or even out of the country and never recovered, at least not in one piece.

If the thief cannot fly or is unable to take off unnoticed, he usually steals as much of the equipment as possible. Then again, this might have been his original goal. Much equipment found in a plane can easily be removed with simple hand tools and smuggled out of airports or hangars.

It's not unique for a thief to steal items from one plane and switch them with another similar plane, enabling him to carry hard-to-trace equipment away from the second plane. The owner of the first plane reports the theft and the identification or serial numbers of the stolen equipment to the police. These numbers will be listed as "hot items," but will rarely turn up, since they are now located in a legitimate plane.

To decrease the likelihood of theft, every aircraft owner should follow these simple steps:

- Always attempt to store aircraft inside a secure hangar or building.
- Be sure that the aircraft storage location is adequately lighted.
- If aircraft is parked outside, always lock doors and chalk wheels. Use tie-down cable constructed of metal that will stand up against a certain amount of cutting.
- Never leave ignition key inside plane.
- If you must leave an extra key with airport personnel, make sure they practice proper key control.
- Make sure your aircraft has adequate insurance coverage.

- Record aircraft serial/identification numbers and affix a special identification number in a secret location on the plane. Also record engine serial number and serial numbers of related equipment.
- Never leave high-value items inside plane.
- Apply alarm systems and anti-theft devices when possible.
- Maintain up-to-date color photographs of plane and equipment.
- Do not store aircraft log book with plane.
- Inventory and check radios and navigation equipment with serial number check list to make sure they have not been switched. (Place your own identification on these items, in addition to existing identification.)
- Know who works around hangars and guards your aircraft.
- Always conduct a flight check prior to take-off to make sure everything is in working order.
- Contact local police immediately if your plane has been broken into or stolen. Provide full identification of aircraft and equipment to police.
- When purchasing aircraft, be sure that all documentation is authentic.
- Be cautious of prospective passengers who request flights across borders or into unknown and secluded locations. This is a sign of possible drug or alien smuggling.

Construction Equipment

One of the fastest growing businesses today is the theft and resale of heavy construction equipment, most of which is reportedly sent out of the country, never to be identified or recovered. Listed below are some very important measures in preventing the loss of construction machinery. In addition, these tips may reduce your liability which could develop as a result of "irresponsible or improper" storage, parking or guarding of construction equipment, resulting in injury to someone.

- Never park unguarded equipment overnight.

- Always attempt to isolate equipment away from main roads and highways to make access and escape more difficult.

- Always attempt to park all equipment within a fenced site that provides adequate lighting.

- Employ the services of a reputable guard service to provide continual security during non-working hours.

- If a guard force cannot be obtained, install alarm systems on equipment or perimeter gates to alert you of possible theft.

- Request police patrols to keep an eye on equipment, particularly noting unusually large trailers or trucks that arrive in the area during non-working hours.

- Mark all equipment in at least two locations to provide necessary identification.

- Park equipment in a tight formation that makes it difficult for anyone but operators to move. A tight formation usually provides only one actual avenue through which equipment can be driven. This becomes time-consuming and too risky to attempt.

- If you intend to park heavy, trailer-mounted equipment unattended for long periods of time, as a last resort, remove the trailer wheels.

- When possible, ask local businesses or residents to keep an eye on your equipment and report any suspicious activity to police and local construction representative. Offer to pay, if necessary. This is a cheap way to get fair protection.

Personal Crimes Of Violence

R_{ape}

Probably the most terrifying and humiliating experience a woman can undergo is that of rape. It is intensely painful and emotionally disturbing, often ending with a brutal beating, or even death. Rape survivors often suffer long-term physical and emotional damage.

According to FBI figures, rape is attempted or committed once every five minutes in the United States. A staggering 109,062 rapes were reported in 1992, and the figures are steadily on the increase. Nationwide, an estimated 42.8 out of every 100,000 women fell victim to this horrible crime, of which a total of 137 were killed by their attacker(s).

What is Rape?

Rape is a violent crime first, a sexual assault second. The main intent of the rapist is to degrade, hurt, and humiliate a woman. Sex, if completed, is merely a means to achieve these ends.

Many states recognize rape as any and all forms of sexual conduct carried out against a person's will, whether the victim is male or female. Yes, males can be raped, by either males or females. However, in this book, we discuss this crime in the context of its impact on females.

Who is the Rapist?

"All rapists are dirty, ugly and frightening." WRONG. I wish it was that easy to identify a typical rapist, but it's not.

A rapist can surface from any level of society. There are no obvious physical features that would point out a rapist in a crowd. But he is out there. Many suffer from severe emotional problems that are in some way related either to their feelings toward women or their relationships with them. Others find satisfactions in physically humiliating a woman, hearing her plead for her life or cry out for help.

For these reasons, never give a rapist an even break. Rapists definitely have mental or emotional problems and need professional help. Nevertheless, don't risk your life while attempting to analyze their problems.

Most rapists are between the ages of 18 and 24, and at least half of them plan their assaults in advance. This substantiates the grim fact that, at the very least, one-third of the offenders know, or have met, their intended victims. The victims, on the other hand, usually have no way of knowing who the rapist is until it is too late. It could be your neighbor, your boss, or the deliveryman.

Who is the Victim?

Anyone can become a victim of rape: you, your little sister, or your grandmother. The National Victim Center and the Crime Victims Research and Treatment Center disclosed through a recent study that 62 percent of all rape was committed against girls 17 years of age or younger; however, victims have been reported from as young as several months, to the elderly in their 90s.

As with any other crime, opportunity and vulnerability rank high on the list of priorities for the rapist. It can happen when the maintenance worker comes into your house to fix your stove or refrigerator, or when the plumber comes in to repair a sink. Or perhaps a salesman has been allowed to enter your home to demonstrate a new vacuum cleaner. *These* are opportunities.

Hitchhiking is another sure way to be introduced to a rapist. Just think how easy it is for an offender to drive around a college campus, resort, or beach and pick up any number of young girls, quite often alone, seeking a ride. This is an ideal opportunity for a rapist, yet thousands of men and women continue to travel across the country this way, many never to be seen again.

When and Where Do Rapes Occur?

Records show that approximately 30 to 40 percent of all rapes occur in the home of the victim. Approximately one-third occur between 6 a.m. and 6 p.m., one-third between 6 p.m. and midnight, and the remaining third between midnight and 6 a.m.

Date Rape

Probably the most widely reported type of rape occurring is that of date rape or acquaintance rape. Neither date nor acquaintance rape are legal terms but they fall under sexual assault statutes of the law.

Date rape can occur anywhere; however, from reportings of this type of sexual assault, most occurrances appear to be on college campuses. Here, daily academic relationships have turned into unwanted sexual advances, which have led to rape.

The co-ed lifestyle found on most campuses is usually friendly. Dorm and fraternity parties present the perfect opportunity to meet new people. This daily and nightly social environment, which includes hundreds of strangers, can lead to what the "Higher Education Amendments of 1992" (Federal Law) defined as "forcible" and "nonforcible" sex offenses. Forcible sex is "any sexual act directed against another person, forcibly and/or against that person's will; or not forcibly or against the person's will where the victim is incapable of giving consent." Nonforcible sex is defined as "acts of unlawful, nonforcible sexual intercourse." Depending on the circumstances, date or acquaintance rape could fit in either category.

In either case, a sexual assault may have been attempted or committed.

What can a person do to reduce the risks of date rape? First, remember that 95 percent of violent crimes on campus, which includes rape, is alcohol and drug related. Second, 80 percent of campus crimes are committed by students on other students. To limit your risks to this violent crime, consider the following:

- Double dates reduce the risk of assault.
- Limit alcohol consumption and prohibit illegal drug use on all dates.
- Don't allow yourself to be tricked into going into an isolated or unfamiliar area.
- Let your date know when you are uncomfortable and demand the right to make up your own mind as to how intimate you wish to become. Learn to say NO.
- Never send confusing body language or signals to your date. Teasing will only lead to confusion or worse.
- Clearly communicate your interest and intentions.
- If on a college campus, don't give your dorm or room key to your date, and never allow strangers into your room.
- Terminate relationships that appear dangerous or risky.
- Attend rape assault prevention courses.
- Report all assaults immediately and seek medical help.
- Accept responsibility for your actions.

Tips on Rape Prevention

To help prevent or avoid rape, practice the following preventive measures:

Outdoors

- Never travel alone. Take a friend or relative along. Develop a buddy system that will help you and your friends rely on each other.

- When walking, avoid alleyways, deserted streets, and abandoned buildings. Never take a shortcut through an unfamiliar area.

- Stay within range of people, where they can see and hear you.

- Always remain within lighted areas at night, and carry a flashlight.

- Never accept rides from strangers.

- Stay on sidewalks and keep away from bushes, fences, and doorways.

- Vary your daily routine or pattern of activity to confuse a would-be rapist. This includes traveling to work, school, shopping, or even getting your mail.

- Always walk confidently, and be aware of all your surroundings.

- Carry a whistle or air horn to blow if attacked or harassed.

- Walk into a store or up to an emergency phone or fire box if being followed. Remain among the general population on the street, but don't rely on them.

- If asked directions, remain at a safe distance, ready to scream and run.

- Use your purse to strike a potential rapist if he attempts to grab you.

- Keep a hard object such as keys in your hand to strike with.

- Use an umbrella or cane as a weapon if attacked.

Indoors

- Make sure that all doors and windows are locked.
- Don't let strangers into your home, especially if you are alone and unsure of the situation.
- Read and follow the guidelines in this book for protecting yourself inside the home.
- If you are inside an elevator alone, and a drunk or strange-acting person steps in, step out.
- Know your way around the buildings you frequent.

Inside Your Car

- Before you get out of your car, be sure you are in a safe, well-lighted location, and keep your keys in your hand to aid in striking if attacked.
- When you leave your car, always lock all doors, close windows, remove keys, and double-check.
- When returning, always look carefully inside your car before entering. If the door is unlocked, walk away and phone police. An attacker could be inside.
- When parking in a public parking lot, keep an eye out for strangers or loiterers.
- Never give all your keys to parking attendants. Remove all keys except door-ignition key. When possible, avoid relinquishing these keys.
- Always have someone escort you to your car after dark.
- When driving, always keep doors locked and windows rolled at least half-way up.
- Never pick up strangers or hitchhikers. Women are sometimes set-ups for kidnapping or attempted robbery in association with an accomplice hiding nearby. If you want to help the driver of a stranded auto, roll down your window and tell them you will call for help.

- Always be sure you have enough gas to get you to your destination.
- If you are being followed, drive into a public place or to a police station.
- If your car breaks down, raise your hood, tie a white flag on the antenna or door, and remain inside the car with doors locked until the police arrive. If someone stops to help, it is better to give them a number where help can be reached and remain in the car.

Public Transportation

- Wait for buses, taxis, trains, and subways in well-lighted, well-populated locations.
- Never board an empty or isolated vehicle.
- Be aware of the other passengers accompanying you on public transportation. When exiting, always remain alert to your surroundings and to the passengers who exit with you. If you think you are being followed, immediately run into a crowd of pedestrians or into the closest well-populated store. Then call the police.

If Attacked

When prevention fails, and you are approached or forced into a rape situation, you still have options. Always remain as calm as possible. By staying calm, you remain alert, and may keep from being seriously injured.

Once you're approached by a potential rapist, try to run away. If grabbed, scream as loudly as possible, blow a whistle, or sound an air horn. Most rapists will try to avoid a struggle. This is the best technique to prevent the criminal from completing what he sets out to do.

Individuals who have successfully escaped from rape situations contend that telling the attacker you have VD, herpes, or are pregnant can sometimes prevent rape, or at least buy you some time to escape. Others pretend to become sick, throw up, or faint. Still others pretend to be mentally ill. Tell the rapist that your husband or boyfriend is coming to meet you any minute. Attempt as many verbal excuses as possible to discourage him. If this doesn't work, two options remain: submit or resist.

Some people feel that by submitting, they are less likely to be seriously injured or killed. Still others, as confirmed in numerous studies, suggest that you're better off fighting back. A study of 274 rapes or attempted rapes in the March, 1992, *Journal of Interpersonal Violence* disclosed that "85 percent of the women who scratched, kicked, bit, ran or screamed did so because the rapist had been violent first." The study also indicated that "while rapists inflicted the same degree of injury whatever the victims' responses, they were less likely to rape women who aggressively fought back."

Other studies revealed that women who chose to fight back were only half as likely to be raped as were women who did not, and they were also injured less.

In either case, it must be left up to the victim to determine what action to take. Don't let any person or organization tell you what's best for you. Education and training can help prepare you to make an intelligent decision, but nothing can replace the value of learning from former statistics about the mistakes that have been made. After all, you are the one who has to live with your decision.

If You Are Raped

If you are raped, what should you do? Where should you go for help? Whom do you tell? In too many cases, the rape is never reported. The victim is embarrassed to tell her family, or fears retaliation by the rapist.

If you have been raped, it is absolutely necessary to get help immediately. Call the police and your family. Go straight to a hospital or your doctor, and explain exactly what happened. If you are uneasy about calling the police first, call a local rape crisis center and ask for advice.

Try to remember as many details about the rapist as possible in order to give the police an accurate description, so that they can prevent him from committing another rape. Don't change or discard your clothing until after the police and hospital have been notified. Don't take a bath, clean your nails, or apply medication. You want to see the rapist put away for good, so be careful not to destroy any physical evidence that could help convict him.

If your daughter or wife is raped, don't dwell on how terrible it was, or suggest that she might have been more careful. The victim has suffered, and is suffering, more than enough. She needs your help, love, understanding and comfort. This is a very crucial period for a victim, and, in order to prevent serious emotional trauma, she must feel that she is receiving support rather than intimidation or blame.

Once you have calmed down and the necessary medical attention has been administered, you must strongly consider whether or not to prosecute. All victims should be aware that:

- In most cases, the rapist is a repeat offender, continually raping women until stopped through force or through the courts. He may even attack you again.
- The rapist must be stopped at all costs. If victims would stand firm and prosecute, most rapists could be taken off the streets for a long time.
- Reporting rape does not mean the victim has to press charges if she doesn't want to.

The Aftermath

The rape victim can suffer a serious emotional crisis. Many women report feeling totally helpless, defenseless, and very vulnerable. It is crucial that the victim receive the support and patience of everyone around her. These are vital to regaining her pride and self-esteem.

Every rape victim should receive professional counseling to answer questions and guide her through possible depression and fear of sex. Rape victims need to be able to talk and express their feelings instead of keeping them bottled up inside.

The victim's feelings and wishes must be understood and respected. She may not want sexual relations for a long time. Let her know that you will help in any way possible. It is important for her to know you understand. Most victims experience no permanent impairment of their sexual relationships. The emotional scars, however, may never completely heal. But in time, with proper counseling, support from family members, and understanding, most rape victims are able to resume their normal activities.

For further information concerning rape, contact:

- Your local rape crisis center; check your local telephone directory for listings.

- National Center for the Prevention and Control of Rape

> Parklawn Building
> 5600 Fishers Lane
> Rockville, MD 20857

Child Molesting and Sexual Assault

According to the Office of Justice Assistance, each year more than 100,000 children are involved in some form of sexual abuse. Many hundreds of incidents are never reported. Approximately one in every five victims is under 12, and in most cases the victim is female; however, both boys and girls are assaulted. In more than half of child assaults, the offender is known to the victim. Many children are abused by close friends, relatives, and even parents. Generally, children are not violently assaulted or physically injured when sexually abused, but fears and emotional problems can do more damage than actual physical assault.

As parents, we have a responsibility to our children to try to provide a safe environment for them to grow up in. We don't want them to take unnecessary chances, but neither do we want them growing up fearing life as a whole.

Among the most important things a child needs from his parents are love and affection, discipline, and the opportunity to communicate. Children need to feel that they can run to Mom or Dad for the answers to their questions. They must not develop a fear of discussing their problems, or they will hold back whatever is bothering them until something gives, usually emotionally.

Although parents should encourage their children to talk with them about anything, children must understand that they cannot expect Mom and Dad to agree with or give in to all of their requests. Eventually, a mutual understanding grows, and love and respect deepen. Parents want their children to believe and trust them, and, for the most part, children do believe what they are told.

Most families are aware of the standard warnings: "Don't talk with strangers"; "Don't take gifts or candy from strangers"; "Never walk away with a stranger." However, they need far more specific guidelines, and these must be explained and understood by all. Children need to know what actions are appropriate, and, especially, what actions are inappropriate. Consider the following points:

- They need to know whom they can trust completely.

- They must understand the difference between games and the perverted actions of a molester.

- They must learn to respect their bodies, and that they have a right to privacy pertaining to their bodies.

- They must not fear coming to their parents and reporting an embarrassing or frightful incident, and, above all, the parents must listen and provide comfort and understanding. The parents' response will usually determine how the child will react.

All children, at one time or another, have made up stories about something they have become involved with. This is to be expected and should be understood to be perfectly normal. However, when a child tells a story about how Uncle Henry touched her under her dress, she should be seriously listened to.

Granted, you don't automatically run to Uncle Henry with threats. The incident could have been innocent, such as an accidental touch while being lifted onto a lap. Sit down with the child immediately, and try to get her to tell and show you exactly what Uncle Henry did that frightened her, as well as what was said. You'll have to decide whether or not the episode was innocent and what you will do about it. You may decide to talk to Uncle Henry about what happened. Maybe you will let it go for now, but keep your eyes open when Uncle Henry is around. You might decide to call the police (if these episodes have happened before, and it is more serious than a simple touch), or possibly just ignore the incident if you honestly feel that the child has been mistaken and it was purely accidental. Regardless of how you choose to handle the situation, let the child know she has done the right thing by coming to you, and that you will take care of it.

Sexual assault often begins innocently, or appears innocent to a child. What starts as a playful touch can turn into a serious assault. Children seldom lie about something as scary to them as this, but it can be difficult for them to tell their parents. After being assaulted they are likely to be confused and scared when faced with the idea that if they should report the assault:

- The molester (possibly a close relative), will go to jail and never see them again.
- They will be injured or killed.
- Their parents will be hurt or taken away from them and it will be all their fault.
- Nobody will believe them or no one cares.

As we have noted, the offender is often a close friend or relative. The child is supposedly safe and secure with the babysitter or Aunt Susie. For this reason the offender has continuous access to the child. In other words, don't necessarily look for the offender outside the family circle. He could well be inside. Children feel safe with relatives, but when something like this occurs, they know that they will see Aunt Susie tomorrow and are afraid to talk.

Love and affection include holding and touching. Children need this contact. Unfortunately, it can be the basis for an assault by a sick, disturbed person.

How many times have you been told to obey your elders? This alone can lead to confusion when a child is asked to keep quiet about a questionable act. "Don't tell Mommy or Daddy what happened. It's just between you and me. It's just a game." This person will usually continue to abuse your child until he or she is caught.

Signals of Possible Abuse

The child becomes:

- Very frightened, experiencing nightmares, and possibly begins wetting the bed.
- Very confused, and cannot sleep.
- Less active than normal and withdraws from everyone.
- Scared to be left alone or with certain people.
- Sick or experiences irritation and pain on private areas of his or her body.
- Curious and asks unusual questions about her body or certain physical actions.
- Depressed and loses her appetite.

What to Ask Your Child

If you believe your child or another child has been abused, ask the following questions of them, or notify their parents or a trusted relative about your concerns.

- Has something strange and scary happened?
- What have they been doing?
- Whom have they been with, and where?
- Have they been hurt or threatened? (Assure them it is all right to tell you.)

What to Tell Your Child

- Whom they may play with.
- Whom they can travel with.
- Who may touch or kiss them, and where.
- Who may help them go to the bathroom.
- Who may help them dress or undress.
- Who may give them food and medicine.
- Whom they may stay with overnight.
- Who may dress and undress in front of them.

- That they should inform you where they are at *all* times.
- That it is all right to say "No, I don't like that," or, "Leave me alone," to anyone making them feel uncomfortable.
- That any strange incident should be told to you, and that you are not afraid and will take care of it. (With this in mind, they will tell you almost everything that frightens them.)
- Be aware of any strangers, men or women, who ask questions or try to become friends; and to tell you when it happens.
- Write down the license plate number of the car of a strange person approaching them.
- Run or stay away from strangers who offer gifts money, or candy.
- Stay away from any of their friends getting into a stranger's car, but get the license number and report it immediately.
- Leave anyone who gets too close and wants to touch them. They should run for help.
- Never go into strange homes or strange stores.
- Never go into a deserted area of a building.
- Never play alone.
- That they can say no to scary or frightening games. If someone persists, they should tell another adult immediately.
- Teach them to scream for help, bite, kick, and run if someone grabs them.

What Parents Need to Know

- The background of *all* household employees — the butler, maid, chauffeur, cook, babysitter, and even the once-a-week housekeeper. Be especially careful with those who have custody of your children when you are gone.

- All your children's friends. Encourage your child to talk about them with you, and invite them over so that you can become acquainted.
- Changes in your child's behavior.
- Where your children are, who they are with, and what they are doing.
- How important it is for their safety for both you and your children to know what threats exist, and the urgency of reporting any incident to the police.

Always try to be aware of how your own actions affect your children. For example, never force your children to hug or kiss friends or relatives if it is obvious they dislike this behavior. When you do so, you are apt to make children feel that they are not supposed to refuse an adult certain acts that make them uneasy.

To help children understand the difference between right and wrong, it is often necessary to discuss experiences at their level. They must understand what can harm them. They do not always need to fully understand the details, such as the difference between rape and attempted rape; they do need to be aware of which actions are considered good and which are considered bad.

What to Do if Your Child is Assaulted

Handle each incident on a case-by-case basis. It is, however, recommended that you:

- Talk with the child and tactfully gain as many details of the incident as possible.
- Report it to the police. Merely keeping the child away from the offender allows another child to become a possible victim.
- Tell the child that he or she did the right thing by telling you.
- See your family doctor or have a medical examination immediately.
- Don't show anger. This can make the child feel at fault or guilty for telling.

Explain that you are very concerned about what has happened, and because you love them you want to help. Remind them that you are not angry and that they are not to blame! Reassure them everything is all right, and that they don't have to see this person again. If they do not want to talk with you about it, they may talk to a grandmother, or to a special friend or teacher.

Do not avoid or ignore your child's stories about any crime or dangerous act. Believe it first, then confirm it. If it is real, assure your child everything is all right and that they did right by telling you. Then report it to the police, even if it involves a relative. This is for your child's safety, and also to get medical/psychological help for the offender. If it is false, don't punish your child. Explain how serious this sort of incident can be, and answer all questions posed by the child. Remind them to come to you any time they feel they are being abused, even if they could be wrong. Never scold a child for coming to you, but, at the same time, tactfully explain the story of "The Boy Who Cried Wolf."

For further help or information, contact:
- Your local Child Welfare Department, Social Services Organization, or Child Abuse Center, which are listed in your telephone book.

Kidnapping, Custodial Abduction, Pushouts/Throwaways and Runaways

Temporarily losing a child in a shopping center or amusement park strikes terror in the hearts of all parents. Most are fortunate in that their youngsters are quickly located. Others are not so fortunate; their children are never found. The number of minors missing in the United States is conservatively estimated to be 100,000 annually.

Kidnapping

One of the most misreported crimes is that of child kidnapping. Kidnapping is the seizing of a person for extortion purposes. Abduction is often confused with or related to kidnapping, but it usually takes place for reasons other than economic ones. A criminal may *kidnap* the child of a wealthy banker for ransom, but a father is likely to *abduct* his child from his ex-wife. If you think in this context, you will be able to discern the major differences between kidnapping and abduction.

Although estimates of the numbers of kidnappings by strangers that occur annually in the United States range as high as 50,000, these inflated numbers are simply not true. If 50,000 children were kidnapped annually, there would be more than 137 kidnappings each day. This total would be equivalent to 220 kidnappings per million people in the United States. On a local level, it would mean:

Area Population	Kidnappings Per Year
10,000	2.2
25,000	5.5
50,000	11
100,000	22
250,000	55
500,000	110
750,000	165
1,000,000	220

When you consider what this would equate to in *your* community, you will probably agree that these figures seem far-fetched.

The nature of the crime of kidnapping immediately transforms many suspected kidnapping incidents into dramatic news stories, often before all the facts are in.

Custodial Abductions or Child Snatchings

Anywhere from 25,000 to 100,000 children are snatched by separated or divorced parents annually. These figures were developed by the American Bar Association and a group called Children's Rights, Inc., both of Washington, D.C. The numbers are considered highly accurate, but the differential of 75,000 cases is strong evidence of the lack of truly accurate statistics.

Faced with this gap in reliable data, many media people regularly cite the top-end figure of 100,000. An additional complicating factor in compiling these data is that few cases are reviewed to see whether custody has actually been granted. In over half of the custody snatchings, the so-called abduction takes place before the courts have awarded custody to a parent. Therefore, no law has been broken.

Custody laws differ from state to state, as do the penalties for their violations. Until more uniform statistics exist, this state-to-state variation in applicable codes will present serious problems. In states with weak codes, law enforcement personnel have nothing to work with. Legislation must come first.

The Non-Snatched Snatched Child

What happens when the court-appointed parent (custodial parent) leaves the area with the child, depriving the other parent of visitation rights? Legally there is little that can be done to rectify this situation. The non-custodial parent is forced to locate his or her child alone, an expensive undertaking in time, money, and emotional wear and tear. If and when the child is located, there still are no useful legal avenues for the non-custodial parent.

In too many cases, the children suffer terribly from the actions of their parents, rarely understanding what is happening, or why. All they know is that Mom and Dad are not together, and they are forced to choose between one or the other. In most cases, the courts choose for them. In some cases, they are moved around the country by one parent to escape from the other parent. Any way you look at it, the children are the ones who lose.

Pushouts or Throwaways

Very few people will recognize the words "pushout," or "throwaway." These labels are given to children who are forced to leave their homes by their parents, children who are abandoned, or who are literally dumped on the streets. Many are exiled for life, never to be welcomed home. They represent the single most unaccounted-for group of children in the United States — some 500,000 cases annually. It is estimated that approximately 35 percent of these children come from divorced families in which neither parent wants them.

Pushouts and throwaways do not become part of the usual statistics mentioned in studies or surveys. These unfortunate children tend not to be reported as missing by their parents. More often than not, parents claim that the child is away visiting distant grandparents or has been enrolled at an out-of-state private school. Sometimes these children are reported as runaways. How many so-called runaway children are actually forced to leave home? What pressures force them to leave?

Although each case must be weighed on its own merits, the following reasons are representative of the majority of cases:

- Divorce or separation of parents, resulting in neither parent wanting the child.

- Remarriage of one parent, whereupon the new spouse refuses to accept and care for a child from the previous marriage.

- The child becomes involved with drugs, alcohol, or crime. The parent is unable or unwilling to deal with the child, and forces him or her to leave.

- The parent becomes involved with drugs, alcohol, or crime, forcing the child to handle responsibilities prematurely. When the child makes a mistake, the parent cannot cope and forces the child to leave.

- The parents are unable or unwilling to handle normal childhood problems as they occur, which intensifies the problems as the child grows up.

- The children are given too much freedom, and the lack of responsibility leads to involvement with social problems (drugs, crime, etc.). Last-minute attempts by parents to regain control fail, and the child runs wild, eventually being forced to leave.

Many adults who grew up with radical philosophies that stressed "individual freedoms," "escaping" from the establishment, or "finding yourself," often with the help of drugs, have allowed this philosophy to affect their childraising practices with predictable results. The 1970s produced the largest number of throwaway children to date. This increase in throwaways also appears to have been directly related to the high divorce rate of that decade.

Will the U.S. throwaway rate decrease? Social change, increasing parental acceptance of responsibility, and lower overall birth rates, are expected to contribute to a decline. Meanwhile, however, uncounted numbers of children will be raised by welfare systems, foster homes, and institutions. Many will fall into a life of crime, and then a life in prison. The final tragic chapter in many of these young people's lives will be suicide.

Runaways

The largest group of missing children are the "runaways." Approximately 1,150,000 runaway incidents, or "episodes," take place each year. We define episodes as the number of incidents involving a runaway child, not just the number of children who have run away, because some run away more than once.

Some organizations have devised an accurate formula for determining the number of runaway episodes a particular location can expect. In a region with a fairly substantial population, one-half of one percent of the total number of people will roughly equal the number of runaway episodes annually. (In less densely populated areas, this formula may be inaccurate.)

Based on a total U.S. population of 255,082,000, this formula translates to 1,275,410 runaway episodes per year. Ninety percent of all runaways return home within a 14-day period, most within 48 hours. The remaining (missing) 10 percent become closed cases, and the child is written off as a stay-away runner.

Why do kids run away? Many will tell you that it is because they are unhappy or that they fear their parents' reaction to some unpleasant news. The fact is, a happy child, one who is contented with life, will not run away. Perhaps the family is moving out of state and the child feels strongly opposed to it; or maybe a child is forced to quit a sports program in order to spend more time on school studies. Other more serious reasons, such as divorce or separation of the parents, can spark a child's departure. Unlike the case of the pushout, this child has the option of returning home.

Long-term runaways constitute a significant proportion of the total. Some may become involved in illegal activity and consider it impossible to return home. Others may have become active in cults, and find it difficult to escape. Though cult statistical data is unavailable, membership in one of the many cult organizations across the country is possible, and could account for a large number of missing children.

It is important to be realistic in examining this national problem. To report on and discuss runaways, it is necessary to weigh the number who return home against the number who leave. To do less is a gross misrepresentation of the total problem.

How to Locate and Identify Your Child

If your child were to disappear, could you provide timely, accurate information to the police and other agencies that could help locate him or her? Being prepared is extremely important. It doesn't cost much, and takes little time.

The following recommendations will assist you in identifying and locating your child. Each child in your home should have his or her own complete portfolio containing information that can quickly and accurately identify them.

- Photograph your children every six months, particularly during their growing years. Any type of photograph will do, providing it contains clear, sharp, facial details. Try to avoid cluttered backgrounds.

- Weigh and measure your children on the same schedule. Include height, weight, clothing and shoe size on the back of the current photo.

- Fingerprint your children. Simply buy a stamp pad with black ink and some plain 3 x 5 index cards. That is all you need. It will be a little messy and probably take several tries before you get usable prints for both hands, but you can and must do this. Don't expect local law enforcement agencies to do it for you, although more and more have taken on this task.

- Determine where all medical records can be located, particularly any x-rays of injuries. Learn how long this material will be kept on file. Storage time may be limited, and you must obtain this material prior to its destruction or before you move to a distant location. You have every right to this material. Insist that you get it.

- Treat dental x-rays and records in exactly the same way.

- Try to learn specific blood type. This information may be available through testing done in connection with medical procedures. Check with physicians involved in treating your children. Some high school teenagers may know their blood type through advanced biology course work.

- If allergies or other conditions require prescription medication, learn the names of the medications, their required schedule of use, and dosages to be taken. Determine the effects if not taken as prescribed.

- Record the size, description, and location of moles, warts, scars, tattoos, and birthmarks.

- If the child wears eyeglasses, obtain prescription data and frame types for all pairs. Know the type and prescription of contact lenses.

- Consult with school personnel to determine any specific disabilities or achievements (in many systems, "Special Education" describes both gifted children and those with learning problems). Sources for this information will vary somewhat according to grade level and school system. Know your child's class placement (sometimes called "Track Level"). If in any doubt about details, ask questions and get specifics.

- Does the child have any distinctive characteristics of speech or behavior? Remember, what you take for granted may be considered quite distinctive to an individual or agency in its efforts to help find a missing youngster.

These recommendations were designed with children in mind, but can easily be used to develop a portfolio on adults as well. Every member of your family should be able to be identified immediately. Adult portfolios should include information such as the following:

- Driver's license number, social security number, medicare number, and any other identifying forms of identification.
- Hobbies, pastimes, or activities and the locations the individual frequents.

If Your Child Is Missing

Immediately report facts and circumstances to the police. Provide them with complete information on your missing child. Tell them all you know about the disappearance, including family conflict that could have sparked this behavior, or any motive or reason for your spouse to abduct your child.

Request immediate inclusion of the case in the FBI-operated National Crime Information Center computer for national availability of information. This can normally be done through your local police or sheriff's office. If not, contact your nearest FBI office with this request — they are obligated to list all missing children on their computer. Do not hire outside services, order posters printed, call a missing persons bureau or organization, or take any other action until you have discussed it with your local law enforcement agency. A "panic button" reaction, and the feeling that you have to do something is natural, but may not necessarily be helpful. Your local police agency may be limited in size, but its capacity for communication far exceeds yours.

Tips for Parents

The following information can help prevent your child from being taken from you for any reason. Parents, educate your children. Warn them of the possibility that they could be taken away from you, or assaulted. Inform them that they should:

- Under no circumstances associate with strangers.
- Never talk with strangers.
- Never go near a stranger's car.
- Never leave their parents for even one second without the parents knowing exactly where they will be.
- Never hitchhike.
- Never walk alone, but always with a friend, and in the light.
- Never invite a stranger into their home.
- Never answer questions asked by a stranger over the telephone or in person, even if they tell them, "It's okay, your daddy/mommy knows me."
- Never take shortcuts to or from school.
- Stay away from deserted building, dark alleyways, and secluded areas, including doorways of abandoned buildings.
- Never enter abandoned buildings.
- Always tell their parents exactly where they will be, for how long, and when they will return.
- Quickly run for help if they think someone is trying to trick them, or get them to come with them.
- Report all important information to their parents and police immediately.
- Tell the police and their parents immediately if they see a friend being forced into the car of a stranger.
- Scream and yell as loudly as possible that they are being kidnapped if they are grabbed. If the stranger does not let go, then bite, kick, and run.
- Try to remain calm if they are taken away by a stranger. Remember, their parents will call the police when they find them missing. Wait for a good opportunity to break free and run. When they are around other people, call for help, yelling their name and address. If they can escape safely, then

immediately get help. Run into a store or among another family and tell them that someone is trying to hurt them, and that they want to call the police.

It is very important to help your children become aware that there are bad people out in the world, but it is just as important that they know there are good people who will help them, too. Do not place too much responsibility on your children. Sometimes parents feel that once they have told their children what to do and what not to do, everything will be fine. Don't count on this. Children can be easily tricked. Consider how confused your child could become in the following situations.

A stranger tells Susie that he works with Mommy and that she has asked him to please pick her up from school for her.

A stranger tells Johnny that he is a relative (aunt, uncle, cousin) who just arrived today for a surprise visit, and has permission to pick him up from school to get to know him better, and wouldn't it be fun to stop for an ice cream cone on the way home?

What about a stranger who says he knows Superman (or any other superhero, or even a TV or movie star), and wouldn't Bobby like to meet him?

Children are very impressionable, and if someone wants your child badly enough, for whatever reason, he will use any means he can think of to accomplish his task. Teaching your children how to react to strangers is important. Realizing that any child can become a victim, and always remembering it, is just as important.

Child Find of America, Incorporated is an organization that is nationally as well as internationally recognized for its work with missing children. A national charity, it locates missing children through investigation and photo distribution, prevents and resolves parental abduction through mediation, and provides public information at NO FEE. It uses trained investigators and professional mediators, and has helped locate 2,358 children in the last twelve years.

To register a missing child, or to report a missing child who has been spotted, call:

1-800-I-AM-LOST

To receive confidential mediation as a parent who has abducted or is thinking about abducting your own child, call:

1-800-A-WAY-OUT

To contact *Child Find*, write to:

CHILD FIND OF AMERICA, INC.
7 Innis Avenue - P.O. Box 277
New Paltz, NY 12561

The following books are recommended:

- *The Runaways: Children, Wives, Husbands & Parents,* Myron Brenton, Little, Brown & Co. *(Hardcover),* Penguin Books *(Paperback)*

- *The Social Psychology of Runaways,* Timothy Brennan, Lexington Books *(Hardcover)*

- *Parental Child-Stealing,* Michael W. Agopian, Lexington Books *(Hardcover)*

- *America's Runaways,* Christine Chapman, William Morrow & Co. *(Hardcover)*

- *Child Abuse & Neglect,* H. Glavretto, Ballinger Publications *(Hardcover)*

For additional information on missing children contact:

The National Center For Missing and Exploited Children
2101 Wilson Blvd., Suite 550
Arlington, VA 22201
Tele: 1-800-843-5678 or (703) 235-3900

The Mugger

The mugger relies on the use of force or the threat of violence to get what he is after. The crime he commits is *personal robbery.* Purse snatching and pickpocketing are crimes of *personal larceny.* In the case of larceny, no threat of force exists between the criminal and his intended victim.

In most cases, the mugger stalks his prey alone. On some occasions, though, he may solicit the aid of a female accomplice (or vice versa) to persuade an unsuspecting victim to retreat to her room or a deserted alleyway. Close behind, the mugger(s) enters, and strips the victim of all valuables. If lucky, the victim escapes uninjured. If he struggles or resists, the mugger is likely to beat him, sometimes into unconsciousness. Muggers often carry weapons and are not afraid to use them. Since a mugger survives on force, the possession of a weapon is a necessity.

The targets these criminals choose all have certain characteristics in common. They may be new to the area and appear lost or confused, or they may exhibit weaknesses such as a lack of confidence or the inability to protect themselves. Obvious victims are the drunks and the drug addicts sleeping unprotected in alleyways or on park benches.

But the ordinary citizen can fall victim as well. Just as the mugger chooses his *victims* carefully, he is careful when choosing *locations* to commit his evil deeds. Dark doorways or hallways, abandoned building, elevators, and parks all pose a real threat to the lone passerby. Once a victim is grabbed (usually from behind), the mugger forcefully searches his pockets for money and pulls any jewelry from arms, hands, ears, and around the neck. Some victims pay dearly when rings or earrings fail to slide off easily. Cut fingers and torn ear lobes are not uncommon. In several instances, fingers have been cut off to remove rings.

Once the criminal feels satisfied that anything of value is now in his own pockets, he quickly disappears down a convenient alleyway. Do not follow him. Notify police immediately, providing the best description you can manage, and don't get your hopes up about recovering your valuables. Statistics are against you.

The Purse-Snatcher

A purse-snatcher can be a ten-year-old or a sixty-year-old. The only criterion is that the thief be able to grab a purse, briefcase, or other package from the arms of his victim and run quickly into concealment. Unlike the mugger, who carefully chooses the time and location for his crime, the purse-snatcher works during the day and during the night, indoors or out. Like the mugger, he too has planned his escape carefully. Once money or other valuables are removed from the snatched purse or case, it is usually discarded.

The purse-snatcher is apt to work alone, targeting bus stops, shopping centers, crowded sidewalks, and other highly traveled areas filled with likely victims. He chooses his victims as a mugger would, approaching only those he believes will not chase him or offer any resistance. Once his meal ticket is spotted, he springs into action, catching his victim off guard.

There are three "methods" of purse-snatching. The "bag or purse opener" is more like a pickpocket. He spots his intended victim, follows, then attempts to open the purse and surreptitiously steal anything he can get his fingers on. The second and third methods are similar, with the exception of the snatch itself. The "clipper," as he is commonly called, cuts or "clips" the strap of the purse free from his victim with a knife or razor; the other "snatcher" simply jerks and pulls it free. These techniques can injure the victim, especially if a struggle ensues.

The Pickpocket

Probably the most sophisticated of all "personal" thieves is the professional pickpocket, who is usually endowed with skilled hands and techniques that include using a newspaper or a hanky as major tools of his trade.

The pickpocket generally operates on crowded streets, inside shopping plazas, and at recreational centers, as well as on public transportation. The crowded bus or subway allows the pickpocket to get very close to his victim without raising a lot of suspicion.

Many pickpockets work the streets alone, but more than a few professionals require the aid of one or two partners. In these cases, the pickpocket, commonly called the "mechanic," selects his intended victim and signals to his assistant. The assistant, known as the "stall," then distracts the target by falling into him or pushing him, always responding with an apology. At that exact moment, the mechanic lifts or picks the victim's wallet and passes it to a third accomplice, who remains in the same position to avoid raising suspicion.

Because of the length of time required to master the skills of a pickpocket, and because much of the cash once found in wallets is being replaced by credit cards, this profession is slowly dying out.

How to Avoid These Threats

- Walk confidently and look alert.
- Never carry large sums of money or expensive jewelry on your person.
- Never keep all your money, checks, and credit cards in the same purse or pocket. Spread them out, and, if possible, leave them home. *Note:* Be sure to record the serial numbers of all credit cards, checks, licenses, and other important documents, and keep this list in a safe place at home or in a safe deposit box.
- Carry your wallet in a front pocket or at least in one where you would be able to feel it being removed.
- Carry your purse or briefcase close to your body.
- Carry your purse tightly under your arm, keeping the straps secured around your arm. If possible, carry a purse without a strap.
- Never leave your purse or packages unguarded in a shopping cart or on a park bench while shopping, unloading groceries, or waiting for a bus or taxi.
- Plan your route thoroughly.
- Travel with a companion when at all possible.
- Take your dog along on a leash.

If Your Purse or Briefcase is Grabbed:

- Never engage in a wrestling match, and never chase after the thief. He may have a weapon and turn on you. Instead, report the incident to the police immediately, providing as much of a description as possible. Also, attempt to get witnesses who observed the incident to provide a statement to the police.

As a last resort, if you are being followed or you feel you are likely to be attacked, toss your valuables into a United States Mail Box or even a garbage bin. Most criminals will not take the time to dig them out. Don't forget to contact the police and the Post Office immediately to regain your property.

Senior Citizens

The physical limitations of many senior citizens 65 or older make them, as a group, as susceptible to crime as children. However, as the quality of life continues to improve through proper nutrition, exercise and fitness programs, the seniors of today want to increase their mobility and enjoy life as never before. Unfortunately, when victimized, too many elderly citizens experience considerable fear and panic, even when not physically injured. Here again as discussed earlier in this book, crimeaphobia or the "fear of crime" takes a toll on the emotional well-being of a segment of society.

When discussing statistics, we know that while 86 percent of crime perpetrated against the elderly is personal larceny, 14 percent of the remaining crime includes purse-snatching and pickpocketing, and reflects a serious problem when it involves injury. Since larceny is the major crime against the elderly, it is particularly important for senior citizens to take steps to secure their homes against crime.

Precautions To Take

- Keep important documents and valuables such as jewelry and coin collections secured inside a safe deposit box at your bank. Make sure that a relative or friend is aware of this in order to help you in the event of an emergency. Never allow access to a stranger.
- Have social security checks and other income deposited directly into your bank account.
- Know the employees at your bank and establish a friendly relationship with them.

- Never answer questions over the telephone about your activities, financial status, family, etc.
- If a person calls attempting to verify your financial status by stating he represents your bank, do not provide answers. No legitimate bank verifies accounts this way.
- Never agree to enter into an insurance or medical program without first verifying its authenticity.
- If you are robbed or assaulted, always report it immediately.
- Many communities have formed groups to help senior citizens reduce the risk of crime. Try to locate one near you.

How To Avoid Crime

- Always travel with a friend.
- Always leave a light on at home when you go out.
- Never enter your home if it looks like it may have been broken into. Call the police from a neighbor's house.
- Ask a friend to escort you home, especially in a high-crime area, or ask the taxi driver to help you into your home.
- Never argue if approached or surprised by a criminal. Submit to all demands.
- Never carry all your money in one purse or in your wallet.
- Never carry a large purse.
- Never place your wallet in your back pocket.
- Never flash your money.
- Avoid deserted parks, buildings, and streets.
- Never go near bushes or dark doorways.
- Always walk in lighted areas.
- Never board a bus or train if it is empty.
- Never go into dark parking lots or garages alone.

Families should take more interest in the safety and well-being of their elderly members. Explain potential problems to them, and help them to secure their homes against intruders.

For more information on crime prevention for the elderly, contact your local police department or:

- American Association of Retired Persons (AARP)
  1909 K Street North West
  Washington, DC 20049
  Tele: (202) 434-2222

- National Aging Resource Center
  810 First Street, N.E., Suite 500
  Washington, DC 20002
  Tele: (202) 682-2470

Submission vs. Resistance: Balancing the Scales

What should you do if you're grabbed and forced to hand over your purse? There's no simple answer. Anyone who quickly tells you exactly how to react to a very threatening situation either gets his information from a crystal ball or really has not taken enough time to evaluate the matter. The possibilities are numerous.

As I have continually stressed, avoid threatening situations whenever possible. But even with planned prevention on your side, the possibilities of facing a criminal, for whatever reason, are there. Depending on the circumstances (mugging, robbery, rape, etc.), some situations require immediate defensive tactics.

For example: Three thugs stop you and say they feel like breaking a few bones because they haven't broken any this week. There is very little talking that will keep them from carrying out their threat, although it wouldn't hurt to give it a try. Unfortunately, you probably can't offer them your wallet, because they're likely to have taken it anyway.

As a rule, if you cannot escape a threat, obey all of the criminal's demands. Remember, you are the only one who can evaluate the situation. As you are complying with the demands, you might decide that your best chance of escaping injury or death is through total cooperation. This is usually the most recommended strategy to follow. However, you may decide to talk calmly with the assailant(s), and use verbal resistance to talk your way out of the situation. Verbal resistance *does not* mean yelling, shouting, or arguing with your assailant. This may, and probably will, make him even more nervous, and cause him to injure you to quiet you. This *does* mean to verbally provide comments that might make him change his mind, such as, "Let's talk this over," "It's not too late to give this up and run," or, "You are only making it tough on yourself."

In the case of a rapist, some people recommend saying that you have AIDS, VD or the plague, but be aware that this could backfire on you. If this guy is six-foot-four, weighs 280 pounds, and is emotionally intent on raping you, telling him you have VD might get him so upset that he will beat you out of frustration. Self-preservation is the first law of nature, but remember, nothing says that you cannot reach the same goal of survival by submitting — by giving in to demands.

However, if after analyzing the situation thoroughly, you still feel that you're in for major injuries and there's a chance of getting killed, it's time to take that last chance for survival, and apply defensive/offensive tactics to overpower your aggressor. Once you have made your decision to resist, what you *will* do is largely determined by what you *can* do. Increase your options by remaining calm, and thinking clearly. The more options you have, the better the chances of surviving without injury. You may even be able to escape.

Your ability to remain calm is based on how prepared you are to face a threatening situation. Don't think for a moment that because you are prepared you won't be scared. Police officers and U.S. military personnel, some of the best-trained people in the world, will readily acknowledge being scared during a conflict. The difference is that they are trained to control fear by recognizing that it's a normal emotional reaction, and that through careful training they will do what has to be done to accomplish their mission. So can you.

Weigh Loss/Gain Factors

There are several points to consider first, and one of them is who else may be with you. If your wife or children are with you when you are robbed, your options are limited. The best bet, again, is to give in to demands, because if a struggle begins, your wife or children may also be injured. It's time to weigh the losses versus the gains. The safety of your family is the most important consideration.

How To Deal With Stalkers

A major problem that has haunted thousands of victims each year is that of a former boyfriend, girlfriend, family member or infatuated fan who follows or harasses them. For years the police and courts were unable legally to prohibit this invasion of privacy. However, in many states today, laws have been enacted to address this problem. These laws, or restraining orders, specifically prohibit a person from this type of activity.

When deemed appropriate by the courts, an "Anti-stalking Protection Order" can be requested. Evidence, as defined by an "Examiner," must show that *a substantial risk of physical harm to another person exists as manifested by evidence of recent homicidal or other violent behavior, evidence of recent threats that placed other persons in reasonable fear of violent behavior and serious physical harm, or evidence of a present dangerous condition exists.*

The court can order numerous restrictions upon the accused, such as denying entrance on land or premises of another with the intention to cause physical harm to another person, or cause another person to believe that the offender will cause physical harm to them.

Depending upon the state, an "Examiner" is usually defined as a professional, such as a psychiatrist, a certified licensed social worker, or other certified specialist who possesses special skills and abilities to determine whether a potential risk to the requester exists. If reasonable evidence is presented by the Examiner, a protection order may be issued from the court, and if violated by the person named in the protection order, can result in criminal charges, ranging from a misdemeanor to a felony.

In the event that no anti-stalking protection order exists in your area, (and even if it does exist), it will be wise for you to take intelligent steps to avoid all forms of communication and contact with the stalker.

Many times, emotionally disturbed stalkers follow and harass their victims because they feel convinced that their victim is "secretly" in love with them or enjoys their attention.

Stalkers often follow their targets to feel strong and powerful. They like to intimidate and frighten their victims because of a jilted relationship or for the lack of attention shown them. Most stalkers have clear motives for their actions, but many require the diagnosis of a competent medical authority to determine the real reason for their obsession.

Even though many stalkers are non-violent, history has shown many who have eventually turned violent. Besides contacting local police for help, you should take the appropriate protective measures as described previously in this chapter to prevent the stalker from interfering with your daily life. Until proven otherwise, you must take this threat seriously, no matter how remotely you feel your life is threatened.

All stalkers must be considered dangerous, with the potential to injure you or another member of your family with little or no provocation. Never assume that because you weren't followed "today" or because you did not receive a telephone call "today," that the stalker has stopped targeting you. Unfortunately, you must always assume that you are being followed until one of you moves, dies, or goes to jail.

Remember, the specific name of the anti-stalking protection order may be different in your area, and the specifics involving the qualifying evidence may vary from state to state. Check with your local county prosecutor for specific information. If legislation does not exist, investigate the possibility of initiating it. Contact your nearest State Representative for assistance.

Compensating Victims Of Violent Crimes

For many years, emphasis was placed on the rehabilitation of criminals, with little or no thought given to compensation for the victims of their crimes. Currently, all 50 states, the District of Columbia and the Virgin Islands actively support these victims and enable them, or their surviving dependents, to be eligible for certain benefits. Compensation varies from state to state. As a rule, however, victims are able to place a claim for medical expenses, drug and rehabilitative expenses, physical or mental disabilities, funeral expenses, loss of past or future wage earnings, loss of support for family dependents, loss of family members (such as child care provided by a mother), attorney's fees, and, in some cases, property loss or damage.

Most states require that to be eligible to receive benefits the victim must:

- Not be related to the offender or maintain a close or intimate relationship with him or her.

- Not have provoked the incident or become a victim due to wrongful conduct.

- Not have become injured through an unintentional motor vehicle accident.
- Report the crime to the police within 72 hours.
- Apply for benefits within one year of the incident.

The offender does not have to be arrested for a victim or victim's dependents to collect benefits. Most states will also provide these benefits regardless of the financial status of the victim; however, some states do require that a need for such benefits exists or that an undue hardship exists.

All participating states have established a set maximum amount of benefits that can be received. These limits, though, do not always apply to certain claims, such as medical expenses to elderly victims or victims disabled by injuries received during the claimed violent crime.

For specific information to determine eligibility for compensation and the individual benefits authorized, contact your state representative as listed on the accompanying chart.

Once the request for benefits is properly filed, a victim can expect to wait anywhere from one to 30 months to receive these benefits, although most of the states provide limited emergency funds, which are usually available immediately upon request. Maximum benefits awarded can range from $1,500 to $50,000.

For additional detailed information, the following groups can be contacted:

National Association of Crime Victim
    Compensation Boards
Attention Executive Director
P.O. Box 16003
Alexandria, VA 22302
Tele: (703) 370-2996

The National Organization For Victim Assistance
    (NOVA)
1757 Park Road, N.W.
Washington, DC 20010
Tele: 1-800-879-6682

CRIME VICTIM COMPENSATION PROGRAM CONTACT LIST

ALABAMA
Anita A. Drummond (205) 242-4007
ALASKA
Nola K. Capp (907) 465-3040
ARIZONA
Rita Yorke (602) 542-1928
ARKANSAS
Ginger Bailey (501) 682-1323
CALIFORNIA
Ted Boughton (916) 323-6251
COLORADO (programs in each district)
Bob Bush (303) 239-1442
CONNECTICUT
Irene Mikol (203) 529-3089
DELAWARE
Ed Stansky (302) 995-8383
DISTRICT OF COLUMBIA
Delores Hollingsworth (202) 576-7090
FLORIDA
Meg Bates (904) 488-0848
GEORGIA
Trixie Stinson (404) 559-4949
HAWAII
Estra Quilausing (808) 587-1143
IDAHO
Kit Furey (203) 334-6000
ILLINOIS
Ross Harano/Dave Ubell (312) 814-2581
INDIANA
Kay Carter (317) 232-3809
IOWA
Kelly Brodie (515) 281-5044
KANSAS
Betty Bomar (913) 296-2359
KENTUCKY
Jackie Howell (502) 564-2290
LOUISIANA
Rosanna Marino (504) 925-4437
MAINE
Joe Wannamaker/Paula Baker (207) 626-6510
MARYLAND
Esther Scaljon (410) 764-4214
MASSACHUSETTS
Pamela Nolan Young (617) 727-2200 ext. 2375
MICHIGAN
Michael J. Fullwood (517) 373-7373
MINNESOTA
Mary Ellison (612) 642-0395
MISSISSIPPI
Sandra Morrison (800) 829-6766
MISSOURI
Connie Souden (314) 526-6006
MONTANA
Cheryl Bryant (406)) 444-3653
NEBRASKA
Nancy Steeves (402) 471-2828
NEVADA
Bryan Nix (702) 486-6492
Gina Crown (702) 588-2900

NEW HAMPSHIRE
Mark Thompson (603) 271-3658
Tara Bickford Bailey (603) 271-1284
NEW JERSEY
Jacob Toporek (201) 648-2107
NEW MEXICO
Larry Tackman (505) 841-9432
NEW YORK
Barbara Leak (212) 417-5133
Lorraine Felegy (518) 457-8001
NORTH CAROLINA
Art Zeidman (919) 733-7974
NORTH DAKOTA
Paul Coughlin (701) 224-3770
OHIO
John Annarino (614) 466-7190
Sally Cooper (614) 466-5610
OKLAHOMA
Suzanne Breedlove (405) 521-2330
OREGON
Gerri L. Fitzgerald (503) 378-5348
PENNSYLVANIA
Marianne F. McManus (717) 783-5153
RHODE ISLAND
Robert J. Melucci (401) 277-2500
Samuel A. Lazieh (401) 277-2287
SOUTH CAROLINA
Richard Walker (803) 737-8142
SOUTH DAKOTA
Mimi Olson (605) 773-3478
TENNESSEE
Susan Clayton (615) 741-2734
TEXAS
Mine Epps/Steve Quick (512) 462-6400
UTAH
Dan P. Davis (801) 533-4000
VERMONT
Patricia Hayes (802) 828-3374
VIRGIN ISLANDS
Ruth Smith (809) 774-1166
VIRGINIA
Robert Armstrong (804) 367-8686
WASHINGTON
Richard Ervin (206) 956-5340
WEST VIRGINIA
Cheryle M. Hall (304) 348-3471
WISCONSIN
Carol Latham (608) 266-6470
WYOMING
Sylvia Bagdonas (307) 635-4050

NATIONAL ASSOCIATION OF CRIME VICTIM
COMPENSATION BOARDS
Dan Eddy, Executive Director
P.O. Box 16003
Alexandria, Va 22302
(703) 370-2996

13

Domestic Violence: Child, Spouse and Elder Abuse

Mary Anne was arrested and charged with the shooting death of her husband, Frank. He had been drunk all week and had been beating her, and she feared for her life. Vowing she would never let him come near her again, she got the shotgun from the hall closet and "stopped him once and for all." Her neighbors watched as the officers led her out of the house. They had been concerned about the loud arguments next door, but no one had called the authorities.

Thus far, we have studied external threats that can affect the family. Now we look at the threats that are created within the home itself: family violence.

Although family (domestic) violence is not new, extensive reporting of it has come about only in recent years. In the past, fear of legal retaliation for making false complaints kept many neighbors from reporting abuse. Now, however, no one can be prosecuted for reporting abuse in good faith. We all have a moral responsibility to report abuse, but our legal status on this issue varies from state to state. Most laws do require that physicians, nurses, teachers, and police personnel report any suspected abuse of children and spouses.

Child Abuse

Child abuse is the continued mistreatment and/or the willful, but not always intended, neglect of children by the person(s) legally responsible for them. Abuse can lead to physical or emotional injury, and death.

In the minds of many, child abuse is limited to physical abuse in the form of beatings. But physical abuse can include being deprived of physical needs such as food, water, adequate shelter and clothing, and proper sanitary conditions.

Emotional abuse can also be a single form of abuse such as neglect — the lack of love, attention, understanding, discipline, and supervision. Verbal abuse is closely related to emotional abuse, since it has an important effect on a child's emotions. Telling the child he is no good or criticizing him too strongly are instances of emotional abuse. Other examples:

- Treating a child differently from other children in the home.
- Constantly blaming a child for problems.
- Terrifying a child with threats.
- Not showing interest in a child's activities.

Sexual abuse is probably the least-talked-about abuse, but one of the most serious. A sexually abused child may:

- Show signs of pain when sitting or walking.
- Become a problem child (use drugs, stay out of school, run away, vandalize, etc.)
- Prefer to be alone, away from children of his or her own age.

Any one of or a combination of these different types of child abuse can be found in over one million homes each year. As many as 2,000 children die each year as the result of abuse. In 1992, 390 children died at the hands of their parents.

The children who survive abuse are likely to carry physical and emotional scars for the rest of their lives. Many will suffer so severely that they turn to crime, drugs or alcohol abuse. Unfortunately, children who have been abused often grow up to become parents who abuse.

Who Abuses Children and Why?

Abuse is found at all levels of society. Many parents who abuse their children were abused as children themselves, and it may not be just one parent, but both. The major cause of abuse can be linked to:

- Financial situation at home. Unemployment, or the inability to pay bills, places intense pressure and stress on one or both parents. When parents can't provide for their family they feel bad themselves, and emotional flare-ups lead to acts of abuse.

- The immature parent who cannot handle family crises. This can include the parent who sets unreasonable goals for children to reach and maintain.

- Emotional problems caused by stress or illness, and childhood problems suffered by the parent.

- Drug and alcohol abuse or addiction.

Generally, most abusive parents do not suffer from some strange affliction, but are, in fact, quite normal. Very few are emotionally or mentally disturbed.

Sometimes parents fail to realize their abusive tendencies. To them, everything is fine. For others, the only way they recognize their abuse is when they seriously injure a child, or are reported by a neighbor, friend, or relative.

Child abusers can be helped. They can learn to recognize the problem and eliminate it. If they are willing to make the effort, 90 percent of abusive parents can be successfully treated.

Although I have talked about parents as abusers, children can be abused by friends or relatives. Look for the following signs:

- Child fears parent, guardian, sibling, or friend.

- Outgoing and friendly child suddenly withdraws from society or becomes very shy.

- Child shows signs of repeated injuries such as bruises, welts, scars, burns, broken bones, lacerations, etc.

- Child's family is isolated or unfriendly; does not associate with others and seems to be "hiding" something.

- Children who always appeared normal begin to exhibit unusual behavior (become disruptive or untrusting).

- Children begin to appear neglected, undernourished, have dirty clothing, are often left alone, or are totally unsupervised.

Few children will voluntarily ask for help or report their abuse. They attempt to hide injuries to protect their parents because they feel they themselves deserve to be punished.

Some feel it's a family matter and nobody else's business. Even in abusive households, strong ties exist, and fear of the possibilities of family breakup can be a factor keeping the child from reporting abuse. Unfortunately, they fail to realize that the abuse will continue.

If a child wants help, he should go to a school counselor, minister, or anyone he feels he can trust. An abused child needs counseling just as much as the abuser does. He must be able to ask questions without fear of retaliation.

Reporting Abuse

If you're considering reporting a person you suspect is an abusive parent, you have probably gathered a substantial amount of evidence to support your suspicions. Remember that every parent at one time or another might be mistakenly labeled abusive if seen spanking his or her child. Use common sense. There is a difference between punishment and severe beating. Try to confirm your facts to prevent an inaccurate report, but do not hesitate to contact the authorities if the child's life is in immediate danger.

Usually, the agency to contact regarding child abuse is your local welfare department. When reporting abuse, provide the following information to assist in the investigation:

- Name, age, and address of the child you suspect is being abused.

- Name and address of the parent or other individual suspected of the abuse.

- When you first noticed the abuse, including circumstances, etc.
- Reason you suspect child is being abused.
- Your name, if possible. This allows the investigating agency to question you in more detail later. You can, however, remain anonymous.

Warning Signs — Before Baby is Born

Some families exhibit abusive tendencies. The following warning signs do not mean that a particular family will abuse their children, only that the possibility of abuse is there.

- A prospective mother or father does not want the baby.
- The mother or father refuses to prepare for the baby.
- The parents feel that the baby will crowd them, or limit their freedom.
- The mother is not concerned about her health or the baby's safety during pregnancy.
- The parents wanted an abortion but decided against it, remaining confused.
- The parents are considering placing the child up for adoption.

After the baby is born, if the parents show constant irritation at his cries and needs, or have nothing good to say about the baby, his future may be in jeopardy.

Asking For Help

Being a parent is difficult. The pressures associated with parenting may sometimes become too much, and the mother or father reaches a breaking point. If you begin to feel like you can't take it any more, you may be in danger of becoming an abusive parent. The time to seek help is before you start hurting your family. Don't lose control or you could lose a child! Consider:

- Talking with your spouse, or other close relative.
- Talking with a close friend.

- Talking with a representative of your religious faith.
- Talking with a social services/welfare counselor.
- Contacting Parents Anonymous; National Center for the Prevention and Treatment of Child Abuse.

Sometimes family separations for temporary periods can help tremendously by giving everyone a chance to seriously consider the alternatives. In some cases, permanent separation is called for.

What Happens When a Report is Made?

When you report your suspicions to the local welfare or police authorities, an investigation is initiated to determine the circumstances and accuracy of the report. The Welfare Department is usually responsible for the initial investigation, and in most cases is required to submit its report to local law enforcement authorities.

If the investigative agency finds evidence of abuse, they will refer the case to the court systems. If no evidence is obtained, the case will be closed or referred to another agency that can counsel the family about a possible problem.

If the court becomes involved, then it generally will order temporary placement of the child with an agency responsible for child care while a determination of future custody can be made. The main purpose of this is to protect the child until circumstances are corrected and the child can return home.

If the court determines that the parents cannot or will not assume responsibility for providing a home setting that is healthy and emotionally stable, parental rights may be terminated. In this case, the child would probably be placed for adoption, but these cases are extreme. The court prefers to return children to their parents following successful counseling and treatment.

If the court feels that there is a problem of abuse, but that it can be worked out within the family, it will place the child under the protection of the court, but allow the child to remain at home if the parent(s) agrees to participate in classes designed to end abuse. When treatment is completed, the parent(s) and program's success is evaluated. If the court finds that sufficient improvement has taken place, the family may return to a normal lifestyle. If the parent cannot cope and conform to this program, the court may then terminate parental rights and place the child up for adoption. The good news, as we have noted, is that 90 percent of abusing parents can correct their problems and regain custody of the child.

Spouse Abuse

Although it gets less attention than child abuse, spouse abuse is one of the most frequent but least-reported crimes facing today's family. It has been estimated that one out of seven women is abused by her husband, but most cases go unreported.

Spouse abuse is found in all levels of society. It often leads to serious injury or death. Police officers report that responding to a domestic disturbance such as spouse abuse may be the most dangerous situation they face on the job.

Women's rights groups across the country are placing more and more importance on legal support in prosecution of these cases. They charge that many police departments classify spouse abuse as a low-priority concern and that arrests of offenders are purposely avoided.

There are several reasons why police agencies handle spouse abuse the way they do. Family or domestic violence has traditionally been regarded as a private matter. Also, a wife may report abuse several times in a row, then decide against pressing charges. She returns home only to call the police the next day with the same complaint. This costs the taxpayers millions in dollars, and diverts police personnel from responding to other emergencies.

Until recently, many state and local statutes prohibited an officer from making an arrest without witnessing the abuse. Almost half of our states now have laws that give police the authority to make an arrest on probable cause, which does not require a warrant.

Spouse abuse, to most, is defined as physical abuse or violent acts suffered between spouses, both male and female. However, because their pride is at stake, very few men file complaints.

Spouse beating may range from a simple slap or push, to an injury requiring hospitalization, or to a serious incident involving the use of weapons. In many cases, the victim taunts the offender until tempers flare. Comments like, "Why are you such a failure?" or, "I should have married someone else" can lead to an all-out argument, or to violence. Some family members even expect to be hit once in a while. Remarks like, "If he didn't hit me once in a while, I would think he didn't care any more," are signs of deeper trouble.

Reported incidents of abuse indicate that abuse by men, as would be expected because of their size and strength, is more apt to result in serious injury. But when a woman decides to fight back, she is more likely to acquire a weapon, such as a knife or gun.

What Can Be Done?

Unlike the victim of child abuse, the spouse suffering the abuse can, in most cases, pack up and leave, although many women lack the emotional or financial resources to do so. Legal recourse is an option, and separation or divorce often follows.

Similar family pressures and stress situations are present in both spouse abuse and child abuse cases. Just as most child abuse situations can be resolved, most spouse abuse can end if both spouses are willing to make the necessary efforts. If both parties agree, professional marriage counseling may save the marriage. Talking with family members or a close friend also can possibly alleviate the problems related to the abuse.

Where To Get Help

- Local public services for support and counseling to battered wives. These agencies can be located in your telephone directory under such headings as "Battered Women," and "Domestic Violence." Call them for help and advice.
- Local police and hospitals.

Elder Abuse

Even more suppressed than child and spouse abuse is elder abuse. In 1992, 1,461 senior citizens over the age of 60 were murdered, some of them inside their own homes, and by their own families. Elder abuse is usually defined as abuse or mistreatment of a senior member of a society. This abuse is not often reported, especially by the elder, because he may rely on the abuser for his food and health care.

Many people are afraid to report any type of abuse, but what makes reporting difficult in this situation is often the inability of the elder to communicate abuse to the right authority. The elderly person may or may not be a relative to the abuser, and often resides in a rest home, nursing home or senior residence facility.

Much abuse is committed on the street when the elder is out exercising or shopping and is targeted by the criminal as easy prey. In too many instances, however, this form of abuse is found behind the closed doors of people you know and trust.

Elder abuse can take on many different forms. It can include yelling and screaming at a person, intimidation, swearing, stealing, hitting or slapping. It can be committed through carelessness or irresponsibility of the caretaker, such as either forgetting to give a person his medicine, or administering an overdose.

Signs of Elder Abuse

- Bruises, cuts and lacerations.
- Obvious pain and emotional trauma.
- Denial of basic necessities such as blankets, clothing, food and heat.
- Denial of personal items, such as teeth, proper eyeglasses, walkers and recreational needs (television, radio, books).

How Do We Help?

If obvious abuse is occurring or suspected, report it to your County Health and Human Services Department, county prosecutor or local police. Take the time to get involved. After all, one day you may be the person lying in that nursing home bed or sitting on a lonely park bench. Wouldn't you want someone to care?

CHAPTER FOURTEEN

The Law and Self-Defense

F rank is finding it hard to believe that his actions of self-defense have led to his being charged with manslaughter, and may land him behind bars for several years.

After a dispute erupted over a pool game, Jim attacked Frank, who was able to overtake his attacker and gain control. However, according to witnesses, once Frank was in control, he continued to beat the other man into unconsciousness. Jim later died of internal bleeding.

Who is the Victim?

> "A skillful warrior strikes a decisive blow and stops. He does not continue his attack to assert his mastery. He will strike the blow, but be on his guard against being vain or arrogant over his success. He strikes it as a matter of necessity, but not from a wish of mastery."
>
> —*Lao Tzu*

Everyone has the legal right to defend himself or herself against acts of violence and aggression. However, you must understand the law regarding "reasonable and necessary force" to make sure you do not end up facing prosecution.

If you were to be found guilty of unnecessary force, resulting in an assault charge, you might find yourself not only a defendant in a criminal charge, but a defendant in a civil charge. The criminal charge is based on legal (public) wrongdoing, which affects the public.

If convicted of a criminal charge, the defendant may be fined and/or imprisoned, as ordered by the court. Legal wrongs can be either civil or criminal wrongs.

The civil charge (commonly known as a tort) is a private wrongdoing which affects a person or his property. If found liable and convicted of a civil charge, the defendant may be ordered to pay compensatory and punitive damages to the victim(s).

Thus a single deed could result in two prosecutions. The circumstances, as in all cases, and the injuries suffered, play major roles in whether the judge and jury determine that sufficient cause was present to warrant a forcible defense.

What Is Reasonable and Necessary Force?

Reasonable is defined as "not excessive or extreme." Necessary is defined as "needed to achieve a certain result; essential." By definition, then, reasonable and necessary force is that which would not be considered excessive or extreme, but essential and needed to achieve a certain result.

Pay close attention to this definition. A consistent definition does not currently prevail throughout the United States. Depending on which side of the jailer's bars you sit, the interpretation can be critical. To learn how your state defines self-defense and necessary force, contact your county prosecutor for a precise interpretation.

As a general rule, most prosecutors agree that reasonable and necessary force is that used to resist what is believed to be an immediate and imminent danger, and the defendant must also believe that the use of such force is necessary to avoid injury or death. In other words the defendant had NO alternative.

In terms of this definition, we can assume that the intent of the aggressor is to cause immediate and imminent danger. I emphasize that this is not your intent, but that of the aggressor. Justifying the use of self-defense and having it stand up in court depends on who is being attacked. You cannot be the initial aggressor and expect to use the self-defense plea effectively in court. Let's look at some examples.

Bill walks up to order a drink at a bar and intentionally shoves and pushes his way past Mike, who has been patiently waiting in line to order. Now Mike shoves back, and Bill punches Mike in the mouth.

Bill could be charged with, and found guilty of, assault and battery, because he was the initial aggressor. But Mike was technically wrong to shove back, since there was no immediate or imminent threat of physical violence. For all Mike knew, Bill could have accidentally stumbled into him. This can become a bit confusing, but it is important to look at the overall picture and consider what the legal ramifications could be.

When you consider the long-range consequences, it can be better to overlook a small incident than to have it turn out to be a big headache. It really is better to walk away or talk your way out of any confrontation, wherever possible. Simply avoid it!

But there are several factors involved here — let's look at Bill and Mike again. In the situation just described, Bill was considered the initial aggressor. If, however, after being shoved back by Mike, Bill attempted to flee the area, and Mike jumped on his back and wrestled Bill to the ground, Bill would now be legally justified in defending himself.

Now, in another situation, Bill threatens Mike verbally and begins to pull back his fist, obviously preparing to punch. Mike does not have to wait to receive the actual punch before applying force in defense. This threat would be considered immediate and real. If, for some reason, Bill were standing across the room and made the same threat, Mike would not be justified in using force, because there was no element of immediate danger.

Use of Force to Defend Another

The same rationale for defending oneself applies when defending another. The same principles exist.

If you feel that a person is in immediate and imminent danger, and he or she can neither avoid nor defend against the situation, you are justified in using reasonable and necessary force to counter the threat. There is no law that requires you to come to the aid of someone being threatened or assaulted, nor is there ever likely to be one. The decision is strictly yours. In some situations, by interfering with an act of violence you may place the victim in even greater danger.

From a different viewpoint, consider what could happen if you should decide to come to the defense of a person being assaulted, and, during the ensuing struggle with the criminal, the victim is accidentally injured or killed. If the victim survives, you could be sued for damages because your actions possibly resulted in his injury. Or the surviving family may sue you for causing the victim's death. Needless to say, there are many things to consider before you become involved in situations of this nature. Usually, a person does what he feels is morally and legally right, and expects a fair decision in return.

Use of Deadly Force

Another very important principle which also must be understood is the use of deadly force, which is generally defined as the force used to prevent immediate and imminent death or great bodily harm. To be justified in using deadly force (it would be wise to consult your prosecutor's office for a precise reading here also), the basic elements are as follows:

First, if a person can escape without risking danger, he, in many jurisdictions, is required to do so. However, in other jurisdictions, you have the right to stand and fight, especially if you take your stand on your property or in your home.

Common sense should be followed in all situations. Even though you may legally stand your ground and defend to the death, it might make more sense to run away and avoid an unnecessary danger. This same principle applies when in defense of another.

Deadly force should never be intentionally used:

- Against non-deadly force.
- When alternate defenses can be used.
- Based on suspicion of activity alone.
- Against a person attempting to flee.
- Against a person damaging or threatening to damage property.

Defending Property

The use of force or the threat of force to protect one's property is generally acknowledged as a proper defense when a person believes that his property is being illegally threatened. However, such force may only be used as a last resort, if assistance from law enforcement officers is not immediately available, and reasonable attempts to verbally stop the aggressor fail. Again, only the force that is necessary to stop the intruder can be applied, and no more.

When You May Use a Weapon

A weapon can be any object that, when used offensively or defensively, assists the user in accomplishing his goals. We know when we are justified in using deadly force. Are we authorized, however, to gain the advantage with the use of a weapon? If the aggressor has a weapon to aid him, then, as a general rule, we may employ our own weapon with as much force as necessary to defend ourselves. Remember, you have the right to use deadly force when you feel immediate, imminent threat of death or bodily harm.

"Booby Traps" to Protect Property

Many different opinions and court decisions have been handed down on the use of the devices, commonly called "booby traps," used to deter intruders. Most states advise that the value of human life outweighs that of property. The general reason for employing such devices is to keep intruders from entering an established property or dwelling — by the threat of, or use of deadly force — when the owner or occupant is not around to do so personally. Here, then, the courts may contend that there was no immediate and imminent threat to the owner, invalidating the use of deadly force. The possibility of an innocent person becoming a victim of a well-placed "booby trap" is a likelihood that must be considered.

Different Definitions in Different Areas

Because of the variances in state statutes and court decisions across the country, readers are urged to consult with legal counselors and county prosecutors before assuming that these definitions are legally acceptable in their areas.

Common
Sense
Self-Defense

W hen All Else Fails

This chapter was written with the reader's safety in mind. It neither stresses nor recommends that a person employ defensive or offensive measures when other options are available. Defensive tactics should be used only as a last resort. However, for reasons only you can determine, there may come a time when you must stand, defend, and/or fight to survive.

Many incidents can be settled safely with a simple apology or by just walking away. A wild two-minute struggle could leave you or another person injured or crippled for life. How would your family survive if they were dependent upon you for support and you were disabled?

When studying defense, we must look closely at offense, for where there is one, you always find the other. Our goal, when attacked, should be to defend and escape unharmed. To stick around and play "Captain America" could get you killed. Escape with the least amount of physical contact possible.

If, however, the assailant continues a relentless attack, you may be forced to turn and strike back offensively, using whatever force is necessary to stop him. The name of the game quickly changes from defense to offense. Your attitude must also change. Survival is everything when someone tries to take life from you. It becomes the most basic of decisions: kill or be killed.

When faced with a committed attacker, try to remain calm and think clearly. Relax, if possible, and call on all of your abilities to gain an advantage in the situation. Use the element of surprise to aid you in your attack. All offensive techniques on your part must be applied forcefully, at just the right time, and targeted at the attacker's weakest point.

When you remain calm, your awareness becomes keen and your reactions sharp. Watch and wait for an opening in your opponent's defense. This may come when he glances away, tries to regain his breath and balance, drops his guard, or switches a weapon from one hand to another. When you unleash your attack, move swiftly and confidently, and, above all, do not cease your attack until your adversary is down for the count! This sounds drastic, but it's absolutely necessary when your life hangs in the balance.

In any confrontation, the two key words to remember are breakaway and getaway. Escape your attacker(s) by using common sense self-defense breakaway techniques. Then "getaway" as far and as fast as possible. Once out of reach of your attacker(s), call the police and report the crime immediately, providing them with as much detail about the attacker(s) as possible.

As mentioned previously, fighting back has to be your decision. If you choose to fight back, then do so intelligently in a manner that will increase your odds of success.

While I stress the importance of communication, not every threat can be reasoned with. A psychopathic killer threatening to break your head open with a pipe couldn't care less about your begging for mercy because your children need you.

Obviously, if someone grabs your purse and runs off into the shadows, let him go, and call the police. But someone who will coldly and deliberately throw an elderly person to the ground for his bus money won't think twice about attacking you for your car or bike. Let the psychiatrist who deals in theory interview the punk once he's in prison. But you'd better plan on expecting a violent attack and decide ahead of time what you would do, and how far you would go to protect yourself or your family.

Let's face facts. There are some people out there who would harass, injure or even kill you for no apparent reason other than that you looked at them. Nobody knows why for sure. Don't rely on any one book or any one "expert" to give you all the textbook answers for survival. You have to prepare yourself and your family to deal with crime, and fighting back is one of several options available to you.

As with any option, you must weigh your chances of success versus the odds of failure. What will you lose if you do fight back? What will you lose if you don't? Ultimately, the choice is yours. Make if count!

Self-Defense for Survival

From our early youth, we are taught how to prepare and react to all types of emergencies and disasters. Early on, we learn how to react to a fire alarm, a tornado, an earthquake, floods, lightning and downed electrical power lines. We are even taught how to react to strangers, but one area that has not been considered part of the normal curriculum is self-defense.

As parents and teachers, it's important to recognize the significance that self-defense plays in developing confidence, assertiveness and self-esteem within children and adults alike.

Once the value of self-defense is understood, a quality program should be sought out by the entire family. Once again, self-defense is used only as a last resort; however, it must be viewed as a viable option when the risk of injury is clear and present. The family that trains together stays safe together.

Find a program that stresses the "KISS" principle: Keep It Simple, Stupid. Complicated, confusing and advanced self-defense techniques are not necessary, and are usually forgotten within several hours of training. Practice what works with your friends and family, and in time your confidence and self-esteem will grow. You will find that there is a lot that you can do to even up the odds when faced with a person bigger than you.

Knowledge is the key, and application of that knowledge will give you the ability to be emotionally and physically prepared for the unexpected.

Children's Self-Defense Programs

How realistic are children's self-defense programs? Should you really expect a six-year-old to be able to defend against a full-grown adult?

When taught by an experienced professional, self-defense programs are not only very realistic, but very effective. First, training that educates the child in the areas of crime prevention and hands-on self-defense should be looked at as just as important as any other classroom subject that is taught in school today. I feel strongly that self-defense education should be included in the physical education class of every school across the country.

This training develops confidence. It not only encourages a proper level of assertiveness; it reinforces the child's right to say no to any abusive situation. Most importantly, this training promotes the proper mental attitude of survivability, even when facing an adult.

Realistically, few children, no matter how good they are in self-defense or the martial arts, will be totally effective in stopping an adult from carrying them off. What is critical, however, is that the child feels confident enough to scream, kick, hit and bite in an effort to escape. By responding to an attacker quickly and confidently, the struggling child increases the chances of being observed, and the incident quickly reported.

What Can A Child Do?

Children should be informed that their number-one weapon is their brain, followed by their mouth and then their feet. They need to think twice before doing or saying something foolish. They need to attempt to resolve a non-life-threatening situation through talking or, in the case of a life-threatening situation, learn to yell and scream for help. Finally, they need to learn when to walk or run away from an aggressor. In the case of a bully, the child should try to talk and walk before fighting.

Kids, if you are unable to simply avoid the bully, then try to talk some sense into him. If you fear that he is going to hurt you, and nobody is nearby to help stop him, then you have the right to defend yourself, but only when no other alternative to violence exists. Remember one thing: rarely is anything resolved through fighting. The problems of the world must be worked out through communication. Use your brain!

Along with common sense, patience, and effective classroom crime prevention education, self-defense training should be considered for your child. You don't have to scare them, just educate them. Remember that there is no single solution to the threats that face children, nor will self-defense be the first option that they should always choose. It's just one more of the many important lessons that are needed in preparing a child for life.

As a parent, fully investigate all self-defense programs and/or martial arts schools in your area before enrolling your son or daughter. Make sure that what they teach is safe and effective. Contact your local police department for verification of the teacher's and/or school's credentials, and always talk with other parents who have first-hand knowledge of the program you are interested in.

How To Fight Back and Escape

Let's assume that you have tried everything possible, including talking and running, to avoid a violent confrontation, but have been unsuccessful in avoiding it. Then you can either submit and ask for mercy, or fight back and escape!

If you choose to fight, then fight to win. No book or video tape will replace the value of hands-on training by a qualified instructor. However, properly presented guidance from a book, combined with illustrations and photographs, can be a great aid in introducing you to effective self-defense techniques.

Seven Components of Good Defense/Offense:

1. **Balance**: No technique, defensive or offensive, can be properly applied without correct balance. Maintain yours and keep your opponent off his.

- Bend slightly at the knees.
- Feet should be shoulder width apart (24 inches) with one foot placed in front of the other to establish a solid, balanced stance.
- Weight should be evenly distributed between the legs and over the hips.
- Keep your back straight, head up, and stay alert.
- Shift your weight accordingly, keeping the center of gravity over your hips. I call this balance in motion.
- Never overextend.

2. **Leverage**: Use muscles properly to overcome your opponent. Take advantage of your strength when opportunity permits. However, never try to out-muscle your opponent. Out-think him. By combining proper muscle leverage with good balance and timing, you can out-maneuver the aggressor.

3. **Proper Techniques**: Combine defensive and offensive techniques. Knowing when and how to react while automatically applying effective techniques is essential to gain control or overpower an aggressor.

Children's Defense Against A Grab

Attacker (A) grabs Victim (V)'s arm.

V quickly kicks A in shin.

V then claws A's face.

V turns and runs for help.

4. Utilization of Aggressor's Power: Go with the flow. Always take advantage of your aggressor's momentum. Push when you are being pulled, and pull when you are being pushed. Through practice with a partner, you can develop the feel of balance in motion, enabling you to take the necessary defensive or counteroffensive measures while struggling. Concentration of power is critical the first time you attempt a technique. Attack the assailant's weakest point, using the maximum force you have developed through concentration.

5. Timing: It is very important to meet your opponent's attack at the proper time to take advantage of his momentum and to place you in a controlled position. You don't want your defensive move to arrive ahead of his punch. You want to stop short of it or slide past it, causing the aggressor to over-extend.

This skill improves with practice. To do this, you must understand components 1 through 4 thoroughly, practice diligently and develop the ability to "feel" when it's right to move.

Another important point is controlling the distance between you and your attacker. You will either want to "open the gap, close the gap or maintain the gap" to make your fighting strategy work. When you move, do not hesitate.

Complete each intended action or reaction. Move with confidence, and after you have picked your target, go for it. When your mind is sure, your body will be sure. Poor coordination and weak techniques are often a result of poor timing.

6. Breathing: Probably one of the most important elements of any successful physical activity is the application of proper breathing. Breath in through your nose and exhale out from your mouth. Explode your breath out with a yell to focus your attack or defensive move. This will add power to your techniques.

7. Follow Through: Once you begin, follow through completely, applying techniques to their maximum potential. Commit yourself, or the end result could prove to be an ineffective application of your technique, and a waste of valuable energy and time. *You might not get a second chance.*

"Defensive" Attitudes of Avoid, Deflect, and Block

My philosophy in life, when faced with a problem, is to solve it the best way possible. In doing so, I choose the easiest and most effective solutions available. Why do it the hard way when I can take the path of least resistance? When faced with an oncoming problem or, in this case, "threat," I attempt to *avoid* it.

If I cannot avoid it, then I try to *deflect* it. In other words, I make as little contact as necessary to overcome the obstacle and escape. But if I have no alternative other than to face it, I meet it head on in order to *block* it or stop it in its tracks.

Obviously, it is preferable to avoid it altogether. If you understand this philosophy, carry it on through this chapter. It can help you in every possible threat situation, as well as throughout life.

Avoid

This is a *passive*, strictly defensive, maneuver, such as turning and walking away or taking another route to your destination. It includes sidestepping, bending, rolling, or jumping, literally, out of the path of a punch or kick. This allows you to recover to an offensive posture if necessary, or to simply walk or run away.

Deflect

Deflection is a form of *soft defense,* where you meet the opposing force, glancing off of it, slipping by, redirecting or shifting balance through deflection of the opponent's power. This includes using deflecting blocks, and tripping techniques — the idea of "push and pull." It enables you to use very little of your own energy while forcing your aggressor to concentrate his. It allows you to maintain control without having it become a "knock-down, drag-out fight."

Properly applied, your assailant will lose his balance, while you maintain yours. If necessary, you can follow up with a solid offensive technique to end the threat situation, or just keep deflecting until the aggressor quits out of frustration.

Block

The *hard defensive* maneuver is used when you are confronted with a direct threat which you cannot avoid or deflect. This is employing force against force. Your energy is being expended in an effort to counter or stop the aggressor quickly and effectively through forceful direct blocks, striking blocks, or forceful throws.

Finally, retreat — move back or out of a threat situation *in control*.

Vulnerability Points

Understand simple anatomy, know where to strike, if necessary, as well as where to avoid being hit. You can take advantage of certain vulnerability points that all humans have to assist you in temporarily incapacitating an aggressor. Review the anatomy chart, and learn where a well-placed strike or kick will drop an attacker (Figures 15-1 and 15-2).

Figure 15-1

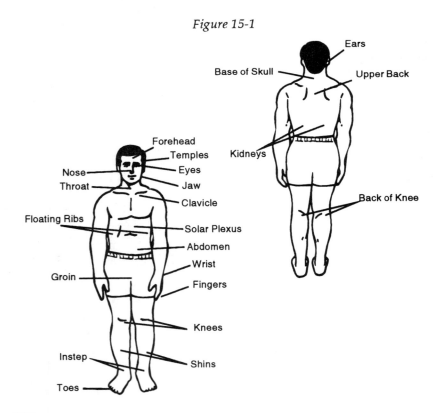

Figure 15-2

STRIKING POINTS

Target	Weapon	Action
Forehead	Punch/kick	Stunning effect/unconsciousness
*Temples	Punch/kick	Stunning effect/unconsciusness/death
*Eyes	Finger jab	Temporary blindness/unconsciousness/ pain/death
Nose	Punch/kick/knee-strike	Blood flow/watery eyes/much pain
Ears	Slap/punch	Much pain
Jaw	Punch/kick	Much pain
Base of skull	Punch/kick	Stunning effect/unconsciousness
*Throat	Punch/chop/kick	Loss of breath/death
Clavicle	Punch/kick	Bone break, loss of control of shoulder & arm
Upper back	Punch/kick/knee-strike	Much pain
Solar Plexus	Punch/elbow strike kick/knee strike	Loss of breath/unconsciousness
Floating ribs	Punch/kick/knee-strike	Loss of breath/bone-break/much pain
Abdomen	Punch/kick/knee-strike	Loss of breath
Wrist	Knuckle rap	Control maneuver/pain
Fingers	Pull/punch/bite	Control maneuver/pain
*Groin	Punch/kick/chop/ knee strike	Much pain/unconsciousness/death
Knees (front/side)	Kick	Break into collapse/much pain
Knees (back)	Kick	Collapse
Shins	Kick/punch	Much pain
Instep	Kick/punch	Much pain
Toes	Stomp/punch	Much pain

NOTE: Striking points marked with * indicate extremely *deadly* points. Use discretion when attacking these areas.

Training

Serious training is required to become proficient in applying defensive and offensive techniques. Study these training procedures to develop and maintain this proficiency. Remember: never undertake any potentially hazardous physical activity without first checking with your physician, and it is wise to warm up your body before practicing self-defense, to prevent strains.

Practice

Training alone is better than no training at all, but with the assistance of a training partner, practice is more realistic. Together, practice offensive and defensive techniques, correcting each other along the way. Work on the techniques that give you difficulty until you feel confident of them. Always work with both hands and feet. Your weak side should be able to compensate for an injured strong arm or leg. Practice defending against more than one assailant.

Move your practice sessions outside. Try to obtain as much "live environment" training as possible, This means practice at night as well, to understand how to face a real attack in the darkness. Develop your senses to perceive an attacker, even when he cannot be seen. Practice your technique in dark hallways and elevators, always keeping safety in mind, while attempting to keep your training as realistic as possible. There is nothing that says practice cannot be enjoyable. The more enjoyable and effective training is, the more a person practices.

Balance

As discussed earlier, balance is one of the seven components of an effective defense/offense. The key is to maintain your balance at all times. Once you have perfected the ability to shift your weight evenly over your hips while moving — "balance in motion" — all techniques will be more effective.

When training, always concentrate on proper balance, and never overextend yourself. Once you overextend, your balance is lost, and so is any technique you are applying.

How can you develop balance? To start with, always keep it in mind. All day long, in every activity you become involved with, think balance. When dressing, expand the simple act of putting your socks and shoes on to improve balance. By raising your knee as high as possible (waist level is recommended) and holding your foot out in front of you for several seconds before putting on your socks and shoes, you learn to balance yourself in this position. It might take a while to learn to maintain your balance long enough to put your socks on, but eventually you will stop hopping around and bumping into everything.

Jumping rope is an excellent form of exercise, as well as a fine developer of balance. Try to jump rope on one foot for a while, then switch to the other while moving back and forth across the room. As you become more physically fit, you increase your ability to maintain balance in motion.

Coordination

Train with both hands and feet during each practice session. To develop your coordination and the ability to become ambidextrous, dress yourself with your weak hand regularly. Put your belt and tie on and brush your hair and teeth with your weak hand. At first it will be difficult, but eventually you can become proficient. These everyday activities will help improve your coordination, and strengthen your weak side.

A Final Word

During practice, always follow through with your intended technique. Never go only halfway because this develops bad habits that may lead to poorly executed techniques during an actual confrontation. Think positive. Practicing the techniques described in this chapter will help you develop a solid base from which to defend. Always seek additional training and instruction when possible. Be flexible and roll with the punches!

Basic Techniques

While studying and applying these basic techniques, remember to employ the seven components of defense/offense. If you are looking for advanced or flashy blocking, striking, or kicking techniques, you may be disappointed, but if you are interested in basic, effective techniques that do not require years of training to master, you will find the following pages interesting, practical, and very effective.

Basic Blocks

The key to a successful block is timing. Practice with a partner to increase your ability to judge distance, thereby improving your timing. When blocking, always attempt to do so with the minimum resistance, deflecting the oncoming punch

There are three primary blocks that should be perfected. They are the *rising block*, the *crossing block*, and the *downward block*. Once these are mastered, you will be able to customize them to meet your needs.

Basic Blocks

Rising Block: Used to block an attack originating from an overhead/chest level position.

Crossing Block: Used to block an attack originating from a mid/waist level position.

Down Block: Used to block an attack originating from a ground/mid level position.

Basic Strikes

As with blocking, timing is also very important when delivering a strike. A strike must also be initiated with enough force to affect its target. Throughout the following techniques, the punch, finger jab, elbow strike/smash, knee strike, and double hand slap will be utilized.

To increase the effectiveness of each strike, target it at the most vulnerable point of the aggressor.

Basic Kicks

Kicks are the most devastating of all offensive techniques, and require greater balance and accuracy than all other techniques to be effective. The kicks shown in this chapter are the stomp kick, shin kick, and groin kick. Even though a child with a basic understanding of self-defense can apply an effective kick, practice should be continued by everyone expecting to use them.

Combinations

Once you are able to apply the basic blocks, strikes, and kicks individually, you should learn to combine several of these techniques to form an arsenal of defensive and offensive maneuvers.

Stance

There are many different fighting styles, which utilize a variety of stances. Each person must find the stance that works for him, whether he is attacking or defending. Every successful stance, however, has certain key elements.

A good stance is one that does not expose a large portion of the body to an attacker, and at the same time provides flexibility and balance. Body weight should be evenly distributed over your hips and supported equally by both legs. This allows for a quick advance or retreat, depending on what the situation calls for.

Both hands should be held at approximately chest level, with your elbows drawn close to your body for protection. Concentrate on using your lead hand for protection or blocking, as well as for quick strikes. The rear hand should be used primarily for power strikes, in addition to blocking.

SIX TECHNIQUES FOR SURVIVAL

<u>Defense Against Wrist Grab</u>

Attacker (a) grabs victim's (V) wrist.

V immediately and with concentrated power snaps her wrist to palm-up position. This maneuver should break A's grip.

V immediately strikes A in eyes with finger jab strike.

V supports herself on A while driving knee into A's groin.

Defense Against Front Bear Hug

Attacker (A) grabs victim (V) from front under arms.

V immediately delivers double palm strike to A's ears, causing him to release grip.

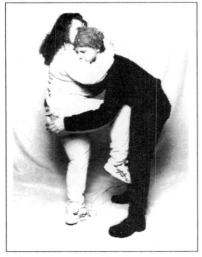

V grabs A's neck and drives knee into A's groin.

V then aggressively pushes A away.

Defense Against Front Bear Hug

Attacker (A) grabs victim (V) in front bear hug over V's arms.

V grabs A's waist and delivers a knee strike to A's groin.

V then delivers an elbow strike to A.

Defense Against Front Choke

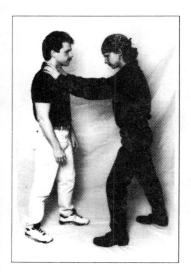

Attacker (A) applies front choke to victim (V).

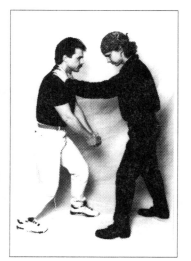

V lowers his weight by bending knees causing A to lean forward, while clasping his hands.

V springs upward striki A's arms inside, breakin A's choke hold.

V quickly strikes A with fists to side of neck.

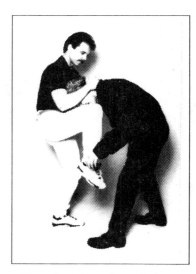

V grabs A's neck and slams A's face into his knee.

Defense Against Rear Choke

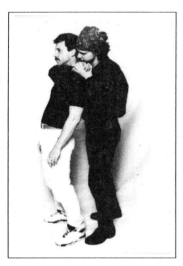

Attacker (A) grabs victim (v) from behind in choke hold.

V raises foot, ready to deliver stomp kick to A's foot.

drives his foot down o toes of A.

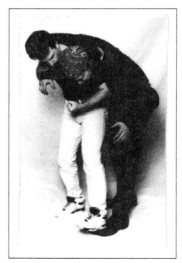

V then elbow strikes A in solar plexus.

V pivots on left foot turning into A using finger jab to eyes.

Defense Against Prone Attack

Attacker (A) knocks victim (v) to ground and sits on top of her, pinning her arms down.

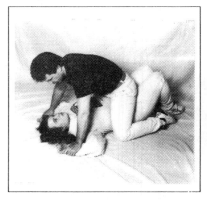

V concentrates her power and slides feet back under knees.

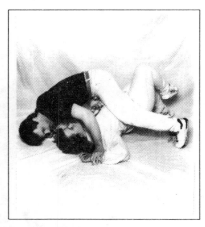

At same time, back bridges upper body and thrusts knees up.

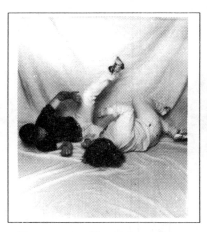

V tosses A off to side and delivers a strike to A's groin.

Federation of United Martial Artists

An organization that was established to provide both quality self-defense training and crime prevention education is the Federation of United Martial Artists (FUMA). Founded in 1984 by Michael DePasquale, Jr., internationally known martial artist and publisher, FUMA is a not-for-profit foundation whose mission is to mobilize the martial arts community in fighting crime through pro-active personal protection education and training and community service.

FUMA fights crime by promoting awareness and by increasing knowledge and developing skills for personal protection. It also fosters positive personal and civic values and behavior among youth through martial arts instruction.

The FUMA membership is composed of over 1,500 leading masters, instructors and students across the country and overseas, representing the full spectrum of the martial arts actively working to keep all societies free of crime.

FUMA's membership includes martial artists who have extensive law enforcement and military backgrounds. They are not just qualified martial arts teachers, but are trained, experienced experts in the area of crime prevention.

FUMA has served the handicapped, senior citizens, students in grade school, high school and college, health and law enforcement professionals and military personnel, and has provided assistance to a variety of community service and charitable groups.

FUMA's ultimate goal is to be able to provide no-cost crime prevention education services anywhere in the United States to all qualified not-for-profit community or civic organizations desirous of its service.

FUMA events and seminars are fully covered in "Karate International Magazine."

For more information on how to join FUMA, or to request its services, address your inquiries to:

FUMA
ATTN: Executive Editor
P.O. Box 8585
Woodcliff Lake, NJ 07675

The following schools of martial arts and schools of self-defense provide the highest level of quality education and training in traditional martial arts and self-defense for adults and children. For seminar information contact:

The Madison Combined
Martial Arts Association
International Headquarters
Sanchi-Ryu Karate
Richard A. Fike, Sr., Director
P.O. Box 441
Madison, Ohio 44057-0441
(216) 428-7008

Close Quarter Combat Skills Institute
Richard A. Fike, Sr., Director
P.O. Box 441
Madison, Ohio 44057-0441
(216) 428-7008

Danny Lane Champion Karate Center
516 20th Street
Huntington, West Virginia 25703
(304) 525-5650

Joe Hess "At The Tower Training"
Joe Hess, Director
110 S.E. 6th Avenue
Ft. Lauderdale, Florida 33301
(305) 583-2737

Falcon Karate
Ron Latone, Director
3659 Johnson Court
Canfield, Ohio 44406
(216) 792-9508

"Somebody Cares"
Children's Programs
Joseph Bonacci, Director
245 Alameda Drive
Youngstown, Ohio 44504
(216) 747-7646

FUMA National Coordinator
Robert Suggs
2507 Culpeper Road
Alexandria, Virginia 22308
(703) 780-2242

Sanchi-Ryu Karate
Jim Miller, Chief Instructor
38255 Union Street
Willoughby, Ohio 44094

Conneaut Combined
Martial Arts Association
School of Sanchi-Ryu Karate
Michael Shears, Chief Instructor
4071 Lake Road
Conneaut, Ohio 44030
(216) 593-3961

Atemi-Ryu School of Self-Defense
Joe Williams, Chief Instructor
11330 N.W. 37th Place
Sunrise, Florida 33323
(305) 748-8023   (305) 777-2989

Woodbury Karate
John DeBlasio, Chief Instructor
18 Sunset Road
Highland Mills, New York 10930
(914) 928-7947

Nick Tarpein's School of Karate
235 W. 35th Street
Davenport, Iowa 52806
(319) 386-4240

Michael's School of Self-Defense
9225 Rt. 14
Streetsboro, Ohio 44241
(216) 626-2004

Continued on next page

Gregory Dillon's Island Karate
Greg Dillon, Master Instructor
8088 Birch Drive North
Newburgh, Indiana 47630
(812) 853-2913

RyuKyu Martial Arts Academy
James Corn
R.R. #4 Box 68
Petersburg, Indiana 47567
(812) 354-3786

Maximum Protective Services, Inc.
Max E. Ciscell, Jr.
63 Birchwood Drive
Transfer, Pennsylvania 16154
(412) 962-3171

Night Hawk Security &
Training Systems
Thomas LeBrun
P.O. Box B-1113
Hanover, New Hampshire 03755
(603) 523-9166

DePasquale Martial Arts
Yoshitsune Dojo
P.O. Box 8538
Woodcliff Lake, New Jersey 07675
(201) 573-8028

Tom Smith's School of Self-Defense
P.O. Box 78
Lisbon, Ohio 44432
(216) 424-1233

Schools Abroad:

School of Sanchi-Ryu Karate
Bjorn Sollenberg, Chief Instructor
Stargatan 16 S-753 37
Uppsala, Sweden

Tony Blauer's Chu Fen Do
372 St. Catherine St. West, Suite #206
Montreal, Quebec, Canada H3P-1A2
(514) 398-9898 Fax: (514) 398-9165

Bibliography

Figgie International, "The Figgie Report Part VI: The Business of Crime: The Criminal Perspective." Figgie International, Richmond, VA. 1988.

Fike, Richard A. "How to Keep From Being Robbed, Raped, and Ripped Off." Acropolis Books, Ltd., Washington, DC. 1983.

Insurance Information Institute. "The Fact Book 1994, Property/Casualty Insurance Facts." The Insurance Information Institute, New York, NY. 1994.

McBride, James T. "Crimeaphobia — A Valid Concept." Published in *The Protection Officer Magazine*, January 1985.

Research & Forecasts, Inc., "The Figgie Report On Fear Of Crime: America Afraid, Part I." A.T.O. Inc., Willoughby, OH. 1980.

U.S. Department Of Justice, Federal Bureau of Investigation. "Uniform Crime Reports - 1991 & 1992." U.S. Government Printing Office, Washington, DC. 1993.

Index